MARKETING

Written by
Louis Rubin

Researched by the staff of:

Wealth Achievers, Inc.

List of Lectures

Lecture One

THE PROBLEM OF DISTRIBUTION

1. *Field of distribution.* – Market distribution involves all those business activities which are necessary to move goods from the producer to the consumer and to make them available in the amounts and of the kind desired. These activities are many and complex. They intertwine or interweave with all other types of business enterprise, large or small.

In many instances, the huge corporations of the present day provide for the performance of the entire range of distributive activities. They conduct market researches, make market forecasts, institute sales promotion studies, develop channels of distribution, direct and execute advertising and field salesmanship, pack and ship products, and in some cases, even operate transportation units. The small business enterprise especially if it is a retail establishment, may appear to be concerned with only a few of the many distributive activities. Actually, however, the small concern must recognize and deal with all or most of the distributive activities if it wishes to be successful. Of course, it is hardly necessary for the small concern to establish the elaborate departments or to develop the intricate organization which may be essential to the profitable operation of the large company. But the large corporations of to-day have grown from the small business enterprises of yesterday largely because they have studied the problems of market distribution in its whole extent. As a result, they have been able to coordinate their distributive activities with those of production, accounting, and finance.

2. *Objective of business.* – Commodities and services are produced for sale in a market. This is true of minerals dug out of the ground, of crops grown in it, of articles manufactured upon it, and of the varied services conceived and performed by men. To bring raw materials from the four corners of the earth and to manufacture consumer's goods is only part of the business job. The finished products must eventually reach the consumer or the factories will be obliged to shut down. Goods are produced or manufactured to be consumed. Potatoes are grown

to be cooked and eaten, hats are made to be worn, and musical instruments are made to be played. The final or ultimate purpose of all industry and business produce or anticipated profits will not be realized. And without the driving urge or motive force of anticipated profits from sales in a market, there will be no extensive nor intensive organization of men, materials, and machines into those relationships which are necessary to perform the productive work of the world.

3. *The beginning of markets.* -In the simplest economic stage of human existence there is, of course, scarcely any exchange of goods. Markets do not exist. The individual or the family produces directly everything that is consumed. Since goods are made for personal use and not for sale in a market, there is no problem of market distribution. A peep at the trading of our primitive ancestors shows us that the market was originally a luxury. Marketing begins with the exchange of superfluous goods. An individual or a family with an extra tomahawk hunts up an individual with a bundle of hair-cord to spare an attempts to barter. The practice of the Australian black-fellows of the present day is typical of primitive marketing. Two parties or groups approach an appointed spot, the men in front armed to the teeth and the women behind carrying the goods. The chiefs go out ahead of their respective groups, and assure each other that they come in peace and not for war. After other formalities the marketing begins. Goods are exchanged for goods. A barter economy prevails instead of a money economy. For example, a boomerang is exchanged for a glittering trinket. When one group's supply does not exactly meet the other group's demand there is a first an argument, and then a regular combat. And yet the characteristics of a market are present. This primitive negotiation takes place at a definite spot where an appointed time an exchange of goods occurs.

4. *The establishment of regular markets.* – Later, as life becomes more settled, the separation of employments, and the specialization of work begins. The individual or the family ceases to produce everything it needs or wants and begins to produce according to its opportunity and aptitude. It becomes evident, for example, that a man who is a shoemaker six days a week succeeds in turning out a better pair of boots than the farmer who turns cobbler but one day a month. As industry grows more productive, markets become more necessary, and are fixed for known spots and certain dates. In many instances, these markets are distinguished by market "crosses," still standing in old European towns. Money appears and is used in effecting exchanges. It overthrows the barter balance, for it is suspended purchasing power. It hangs over the market "to be used, nobody knows when, or where, or for what." And yet, for years the markets remain local in the main. Most exchanges are made directly between the producer and the consumer, although as time goes on, many men break away from cultivation and fabrication to become exclusively handlers of goods, buying from all and selling all.

5. *The effect of specialization and large-scale production.* - Then the possibilities of large-scale manufacture present themselves. Commercial needs and economic conditions favorable for experimentation call forth inventive genius. New machines and new sources of power develop productive capacities with amazing rapidity. The specialization of labor

continues, but there is even more specialization by machines. Territorial specialization also proceeds at an astounding rate. When communities specialize and make the products for which they are best fitted, either through their natural endowment or through the development of special services and facilities, productivity rapidly increases. Moreover, the people of all localities and communities become interdependent and cooperative, like workers in a single plant. The Massachusetts shoemaker, the British miner, the Ohio machinist, the Southern cotton-grower, and the Minnesota wheat farmer are all dependent one upon the other. Markets, once merely local institutions, become nation-wide and world-wide. Competition to push back limiting market frontiers grows in intensity as production speeds up. It appears almost as though the looms weave cloth more rapidly than we can wear it out, that the farmers raise crops in greater abundance than we can consume them, and that machines and assembly lines pour goods into the world markets faster than they can be absorbed.

6. *The gap between producer and consumer.* -Because of the tendency toward large-scale production and geographical specialization a wide gap develops between the producer or manufacturer and the ultimate consumer. In our modern economic life, the great bulk of production is for the general market rather than know individuals. Producer and consumer do not usually come directly into contact with each other. It is only on very rare occasions that the skilled craftsman or the farmer acts as a salesman. Most industrial workers make or help to make goods which others will sell to unknown customers, many of whom may be living on other continents. In the stock of a small retail store there can be found goods from practically every state in the Union and from many foreign lands. An ultimate consumer in California wears a suit of clothes made in Rochester, New York, out of cloth manufactured in Atlanta, Georgia, from wool imported from South America and colored with dyes brought from Switzerland. In order that this ultimate consumer may be comfortably and neatly clothed, the manufacturer of this suit has drawn upon the resources of at least three continents. In addition, he and other distributive agencies have performed a whole group of service activities. Certainly the problem of getting goods to the consumer has become highly complicated and demands the services of experts possessing the highest grade of business ability. Market distribution is no longer a butterwoman's job.

7. *Distribution the business problem of the present.* – An extremely elaborate system has developed for the purpose of bridging the gap between the farm, the mine, and the factory, and thousands of business organizations and households whose needs and wants these producing agencies must supply. The function of market distribution has become highly specialized and is now distinctly separated from the function of physical production. When oil operations welcome a material drop in oil production, when farmers grow "bumper" crops only to discover that they must market them at a loss, when manufacturers see their distribution costs mount so high that they offset production savings, when wholesalers and retailers find it necessary to buy from "hand to mouth" in order to increase their rate of turnover to "the point which enables them to survive" -it must be evident that we are living in an "Age of Distribution," an age pf perplexing problems and challenging costs. Moreover, it is entirely likely that these problems will increase in importance. The more advanced out civilization becomes, the more likely to put upon *service* and *time*, and the more complicated will be the problem of distribution.

8. *Definition of the term distribution.* -In order to understand this problem of distribution it is necessary to resolve it into its component parts or elements. However, before we proceed to an analysis of distributive activities we need to be sure of certain of our terms. The word distribution is used here not in the special and technical sense in which it is applied in pure economic science, the sense of income distribution. Ordinarily, the economist divides his field of study into three parts, production, distribution and consumption. He defines production as the process of creating elementary, form, time and place utilities. Under such a definition, what is called market distribution in this text falls under the head of production. To the economist, distribution is the process by which the total income of the entire nation is apportioned to labor, capital, land and management. In this sense, distribution deals with rent, wages, interest, and profit, their nature and their relationship one to another. The business man, however, speaks of production in the sense of the creation of form utilities alone, and of distribution as all the activities of getting goods from those who are primarily responsible for the form of the commodity to those who will ultimately consume the commodity. In this text, distribution will be used in its business meaning rather than in its special economic sense.

9. *The distributive functions.* -In making a purchase, the consumer must decide upon the type of goods, the particular brand, grade or unit to be purchased, and the particular vendor to be patronized. In this whole process he is influenced by the extent to which distributors carry out their responsibilities. These responsibilities or activities are called the distributive functions. They include standardization, storing, transporting, risk-bearing, financing, assembling or purchasing, and demand-creating or selling. Two of these activities, risk-bearing and financing, underlie all business activity, and therefore, they are not exclusively the problems of distribution. Standardization (grading and sorting), storing and transporting are physical matters, in the main, and are sometimes set apart from the more purely *marketing* functions of purchasing and selling. In fact, a definite distinction is sometimes made between the terms "distribution" and "marketing." The former is often said to be an all-inclusive term which involves all the functions listed above, while the latter is often rather specially restricted to the activities of purchasing and selling.

10. *Standardization.* -The function of standardization involves the adoption of definite rules for classifying commodities into uniform groups. These standards or rules may be based upon a variety of factors such as size, shape, strength, chemical content, flavor, moisture, method of packing, etc. The actual dividing or sorting in accordance with these standards or rules is grading. The standards or rules which are used in grading may be fixed by public authority or by private initiative. Common or public standards are usually established and promulgated by the state or federal governments. They tend to do away with distinctiveness as regards the output of any one producer because they frequently result in the mixing of goods of similar types and grades so that the identity of individual lots is lost. They make it possible to sell goods by description (grade) rather than by sample or inspection. Private standards are used to make the units of a product uniform, to provide easy identification, and to indicate distinctiveness when compared with competing products. These standards are represented by brands or trademarks which are known to the market through advertising and personal salesmanship. Grading may be performed as near as possible to the point of production or manufacture.

11. *Storage.* – There is almost always a "lag" between production and consumption which makes storage highly essential. Goods must be stored until consumers are ready to use them because the consumption of most products is fairly even and continuous while production is often intermittent. The huge elevators in which grain is held until the millers buy, the large oil tanks, the warehouses in which manufacturers store raw materials and in which they accumulate their finished products, the warehouse in which jobbers and wholesalers keep their complex variety of supplies, the storerooms, shelves, counters and display cases of the retailer-all are parts of the necessary storage system. In general, there is a need for three kinds of storage: common, special, and cold. Common warehouses provide storage for non-perishable products and are built merely to protect them and prevent them from being wasted. Semi-perishable products are stored in special warehouses which may be equipped with air-circulating and temperature-controlling devices. Cold storage warehouses are furnished for perishables like green vegetables, butter, eggs, meats, and so on, and are equipped to provide temperatures at or below freezing.

12. *Transportation or traffic control.* - Even in the case of the simplest marketing mechanism, the transportation function is involved and must be performed by either the buyer or the seller. Transportation or traffic control includes a variety of sub-functions such as proper packing and loading, the selection of suitable routes, the securing of favorable rates, the effective use of terminal facilities, and the study and control of trucking, draying, or delivery systems. The cost of transportation is often so high that it limits the geographical bounds within which the produce can be marketed. The cost of performing the original haul, carried on largely by wagons and motor trucks, the intermediate haul, accomplished by the railroads and steamships, and the final haul by wagons and trucks, has a very vital effect on the problem of reaching the consumer.

13. *Risk-taking.* -At all stages of the marketing process there are certain risks which must be assumed by the seller, buyer, middleman, or risk-bearing specialist. In general, these risks are of three types: Definite risks, indefinite risks, and price risks. Definite risks are the risks of physical losses, and consequent money losses, through fire, flood, sprinkler leakage, tornado, hail, theft, etc. Most of these risks can be passed over to professional risk takers, the insurance companies. However, the insurance premiums which must be paid add to the cost of doing business and the indemnities paid over to the insurer seldom compensate completely for the loss sustained. Indefinite risks are the risks of losses caused by deterioration, style changes, and the like. These risks must be borne by the owner of the goods and can be minimized only by the exercise of good business judgement in buying and selling. Price risks are similar. Losses may be sustained because of changes in market prices. These losses must be borne by the owner of the goods. They cannot be passed on to others except through hedging which is possible in organized commodity exchanges where future trading is permitted.

14. *Financing.* -Financing, too, is an important function which is fundamental to the whole process. Goods are produced or manufactured, stored, and transported in the assumption that they will be purchased and paid for in money. On this assumption credits may be secured during the period of transportation and while goods are in storage. The task of securing these credits is an important function of the producer, manufacturer, or middleman. Practically every

series of ownership transfer necessary financing, and financing quite naturally increases in importance with the length of time which elapses between production and consumption.

15. *Assembling or purchasing.* -Three types pf purchasing or assembling activities are important. There is first the assembly of like goods for the purpose of obtaining a sufficient quantity of goods under one control for economical operation. This is the type of assembly which interests the car-lot shipper, the local grain elevator owner, the cotton broker, the grain broker, and similar operators. Next there is the assembly which is performed for the immediate purpose of obtaining raw materials, fabricating goods, accessory goods, and installation equipment in the amounts, of the kind, and at the price to make possible economical manufacturing. This is the type of assembly in which the purchasing agent of the manufacturer is engaged. Finally, there is assembly for the purpose of obtaining a variety and quantity of goods sufficient to meet the convenience of buyers and to make economical operation possible. This, in turn, is the province of the purchasing agent for the jobber or wholesaler of consumers' goods, and of the retailer. In all types, the efficient performance of this function depends upon a thorough knowledge of market supply, market demand, market prices, and sources of production, an economical and effective system for filling and following up orders, and a continuous check of stocks on hand.

16. *Demand creating or selling.* -Selling or demand creating activities in some form are involved in the distribution of every commodity. Sales are made on three bases, by inspection, by sample, and by description. Of the three methods, sales made on the basis of description are the least costly. But not all products lend themselves to sale by description. It may be impossible to sell a carload of potatoes by description or even by sample. The purchaser may insist upon inspection. On the other hand, it may be perfectly possible to sell a watch by description alone. The two principle sales methods utilized are advertising and personal salesmanship. Either may be used alone, but both are generally employed in some carefully planned combination. The steps involved in demand creating and making a sale are: Advising the buyer as to kind and quality of goods, and where they can be secured, creating an effective desire, and securing an agreement as to price and terms.

These principal distributive activities or functions are performed by the producer and by various types of middlemen. Accordingly, the next question is concerned with who middlemen are and with what they do.

17. *Definition of middlemen.* -Middlemen are individuals, firms, or corporations that stand between prime producers and ultimate consumers and that specialize in the transfer of title to goods and in the performance of other essential marketing services. These individuals, firms, or corporations, are in business for themselves and attempt to conduct their enterprises in a way not only to be paid for the costs of their services, but also to make a profit in addition for the risks they assume. Salesmen are not middlemen. They are excluded according to the definition because they are not in business for themselves, do not assume the risks of an entrepreneur, and do not receive any profit, as such, from their sales. Hence, a manufacturer who sells his products exclusively through salesmen who call upon ultimate consumers from door to door, is not selling through middlemen.

18. *Classification of middlemen.* -All middlemen may be classified according to their relationship to the transfer of title to goods. In fact, the relationship of middlemen to the ownership of goods and to the transfer of title to goods is one of the most logical and useful factors in defining the position of any group of middlemen, both from a legal and an economical point of view. On this basis, middlemen may be classified as merchants and as functional middlemen.

19. *Merchant middlemen.* – Those middlemen who buy goods outright, and thus take title to the goods are called merchants. This class of middlemen generally performs all or most of the distributive functions. This class of middlemen generally performs all or most of the distributive functions. Wholesale receivers, jobbers, and retailers are the most important members of the merchant class of middlemen.

20. *Functional middlemen.* -Those middlemen who assist directly in bringing about a transfer of title to goods, are called functional middlemen. This class of middlemen generally specializes in the performance of a limited number of the marketing functions, one of which has reference to the transfer of title through assembling or selling, or both. Selling agents, brokers, and commission men are the most important members of the functional class of middlemen. There is a tendency in some cases to include in the classification of functional middlemen other individuals, firms, corporations specializing in the performance of a part or all of the work involved in some one type of market service. Such agencies as railroads, cold storage plants, public warehouses, inspectors, graders, banks and insurance companies, by acting in some specialized capacity facilitate certain distributive activities for the producer, the middleman, and the consumer. They are not *bona fide* middlemen, however, and they should not be thus classified, even in the functional group, for they render no direct assistance in the transfer of title.

21. *The problem with distribution.* -The problem of distribution for a particular distributor is the problem of determining upon the extent to which the various distributive functions must be carried out, and of deciding who can carry them out most effectively and most economically. In some cases, it is becoming possible and economical to do without middlemen entirely in the process of distribution. In others a smaller number of middlemen are being used. But these facts do not mean that the middlemen are disappearing from modern business nor that the distributive functions are being eliminated. The producer in most cases uses the services of middlemen. This is an age of indirect exchange of goods is really much simpler and much less expensive than a plan under which every producer tries to deal directly with the final consumer. We are all specialists in one narrow groove in industry, and we have no time to hunt out for ourselves all the other specialists whose goods we need. Usually individual producers cannot perform the marketing functions effectively and economically without calling upon the middleman in some degree.

22. *Criticism of the middleman.* -The middleman is an important figure in the distribution of most goods. Hence, when the present distributing system is criticized, the middleman bears the burden of the attack. Some of this fault-finding is justifies, but much of it is founded on a misunderstanding of who the middleman is and what he does. The word "middleman" is often incorrectly applied to mean only the jobber or other type of wholesaler. Of

course, the jobber is a middleman, but so, too, is the retailer. When critics generalize about "middlemen" they are talking about no one group of distributors but about every individual and every factor standing between the manufacturer and the consumer. Moreover, the middleman exists because he has been called into existence, on the one hand, by the necessities of large-scale and specialized production and, on the other hand, by the necessities of consumers, also highly specialized in their activities and constantly demanding more and more in the way of service which the distant manufacturer, in most cases, must rely upon the middleman to give. Obviously, from time to time, some middlemen will be eliminated from the distributive system. The functions of others will change. But it is safe to say that the complete elimination of middlemen as a class is an economic impossibility in our complex industrial system.

Indeed, whether or not a particular middleman may be economically eliminated in a distributive situation rests on answers to these questions: (a) Is the middleman performing useless functions? (b) Is he performing necessary functions in an inefficient and uneconomical manner? (c) Can producer, consumer or other middlemen perform the necessary functions more effectively and economically?

THE FUNCTION OF MARKETING

1. *Original and present meaning of distribution.* -The possibility of setting up a distinction between the term "distribution" and the term "marketing" has been suggested in the preceding chapter. Formerly, a definite distinction was common. "Distribution" meant originally a literal and physical dividing or parceling out, a separation by class or location, and nothing more. Only in an extension of the natural meaning is "distribution anything but physical. Promotion methods that figuratively move goods by persuasion through pictures and print, are not matters of "distribution" in the fundamental sense of the word. However, in its present business usage, "distribution" has come to mean matters of *promotion* as well as matters of *motion.* It is now a broad term which includes all of the functions that have been briefly described in the foregoing chapter.

2. *Changes in the meaning of marketing.* – Marketing, too, has often been limited in definition to selling by means of the distribution of such ideas about goods as will arouse desire for the goods and cultivate willingness on the part of the consumers to pay the price and to make the required effort to secure the goods. To many minds, "marketing, is still precisely synonymous with selling, and in many business enterprises nothing exists in the way of marketing organization beyond the sales department. Of late, however, there has sprung up a growing realization that marketing involves something above and beyond mere salesmaking. In

addition to personal salesmanship and advertising it comprises research, forecasting, planning and other development activities. Discerning experts have discovered that it is more important to coordinate production schedules with carefully-determined sales possibilities than it is to develop a huge volume of output and unload an impossible selling upon an efficient sales department already doing its best. Marketing, then, has broadened out in its scope so that in addition to touching the physical activities of distribution at many points, it reaches back into product manufacture as well.

3. *Distinction between physical and non-physical activities*. -The physical activities connected with distribution involve the actual handling of the goods. Those of non-physical character concern the research and promotion methods employed to determine markets, arouse consumer demand and develop sales possibilities. It is obvious that in their extended meanings both "distribution" and "marketing "are synonymous terms, including the activities of physical supply as well as those of demand creation. These two types of activity are interdependent. Consumer demand, when aroused, has no profit-making value unless provision is made "foe satisfying it by actual transfer of the goods through one or more of the available agencies." Nevertheless, it is convenient to keep in mind a distinction between the physical distributive or marketing activities and those of a non-physical type. The emphasis necessary on one type of activity as opposed to the other depends upon the kinds of goods that a particular enterprise produces and wishes to place in the hands of the consumer. One group or class of goods may demand particular attention to physical distributive problems while another may demand the same degree of attention to the non-physical marketing problems. Moreover, most of the criticism of modern distribution or marketing is directed against the non-physical activities, and with good reason. These activities, of course, are more controllable than the physical distributive activities. There is little excuse for allowing their costs too equal, exceed, or completely counterbalance savings brought about by economics in manufacturing. Finally, even to-day, whenever the term "marketing" is used in a restricted sense rather than in its extended meaning, the intent is to refer to the non-physical activities.

4. *Steps in scientific marketing practice*. -Excluding from consideration, for the moment, such physical activities as transporting and storing and such general business activities as risk-taking and financing, we find the list of non-physical marketing activities covers: (a) market research, (b) market forecasting, (c) the formulation of definite market policies with respect to product, price, trade channels, dealers and consumers, (d) market planning, (e) the effective and economical direction and control of advertising, and (f) the effective and economical direction and control of personal salesmanship. These activities are sometimes called the fundamental steps in scientific marketing practice.

5. *Staff and line marketing activities*. -In the foregoing list of fundamental steps in scientific marketing practice there are two distinct types of activities. These activities may be classified as staff and line marketing activities. The line activities are concerned with the adoption and approval of plans, with the issuance of orders, with the maintenance of discipline and morale, and with the execution of plans. The staff activities involve study, research, analysis, and the presentation of advisory recommendations.

In the group of six non-physical marketing activities-the direction and control of advertising, and the direction and control of personal salesmanship. Market research, market forecasting, market-policy formulation and market planning are primarily staff activities. If we add the physical activities of storing and transporting, we include two other line activities.

6. *Principal classes of vendible goods.* -The six activities connected with scientific marketing practice may be carried on by the producer or manufacturer or by the individual middleman, or they may be split up between the producer or manufacturer and different types of middlemen. In some cases, the individual producer or manufacturer and the individual middleman will not be able to handle these activities because of the nature of the product. Accordingly, the characteristics of the principal product groups or classes should be studied to ascertain the relative importance of the physical and non-physical distributive or marketing activities and to note in particular the limitations on those of the several non-physical marketing activities listed above.

Although the variety and complexity of goods and commodities on the market seem endless, products can be roughly classified with comparative ease. The principal groups or classes of goods are: Agricultural products, raw-materials, technical or industrial commodities, consumers' manufactured goods, and services and rights.

7. *Agricultural products.* -The farm produces a large portion of the world's supply of vendible commodities. Wheat, cotton, barley, oats, rice, flax, rye, corn, tobacco, and fruits and vegetables are typical primary farm products. Among the secondary farm products are livestock and dairy products. Some of these products like fruits, vegetables, milk, cream and eggs, are ready for consumption when they leave the farm. Others, like the grains, livestock, and textile fibers must pass through one or more manufacturing processes before they are ready for consumption.

8. *Distributive factors relating to agricultural goods.* -The marketing of agricultural goods is highly complicated by the following factors: agricultural products are produced on a small scale by a very large number of producers, agricultural production is very largely seasonal in character, a large portion of farm production is perishable, agricultural production varies greatly in quality and quantity from season to season. As a result of these factors the physical functions of assembling, transportation control, grading, and storing are exceedingly important. Since the points of production and consumption are widely separated, agricultural products pass through various types of markets. These markets are usually classified as: Local markets (at country points), primary wholesale markets (at central concentration points), terminal markets or secondary wholesale markets (at central distribution points), and retail outlets (at points of consumption). In the local markets are found the following types of middlemen: Local buyers, car-lot shippers, country-store buyers and shippers, traveling buyers, traveling brokers, and cooperative shippers. In the primary wholesale markets are the brokers, commission men, auction companies, jobbers, car-lot wholesalers, and cooperative selling agents. In general, these same middlemen are typical of the terminal or secondary wholesale markets. Among the retail outlets are the grocery, meat, dairy product, and fruits and vegetable stores, the public retail markets, the chain and the cooperative food product retail establishments.

9. *Limitations on use of non-physical activities*. -The individual farm producer can make very little use of the six non-physical activities involved in scientific marketing procedure. Market analysis and market forecasting are available to him only to a limited extent. He can adopt and use certain definite policies of production but he cannot package or identify his products by brand on a large scale. It is impossible for him to select his own distribution channels irrespective of existing marketing middlemen. He cannot enforce particular price policies because he is a small producer and must take practically what the assembling middlemen offer. Neither can he work out dealer or consumer policies. He can make very little use of effective personal salesmanship and practically no use of advertising. Only by combining with other producers in cooperative marketing associations can he apply these techniques intensively or extensively. The agricultural middlemen can do more, of course, but he, too, is limited by the fact that essentially he is a small handler in comparison with the total volume of almost exactly similar production.

10. *Raw-materials*. -The second group or class of products includes all those raw-material commodities other than primary farm products. The extractive products such as coal, iron ore, zinc, copper, and lead belongs to this group. Here, too, some products, such as coal, go directly to the household for consumption, while iron ore, copper, zinc and lead must be processed. But even in the case of coal, a very large tonnage becomes raw material for industry and is consumed in the productive process. In this second group belong also fabricating goods. These are goods which have already been processed to some extent but which are still considered raw materials and must go through additional manufacturing operations before they are ready to be consumed. Sheet iron, structural steel, hides, textiles, and cut lumber are illustrative of fabricating goods.

11. *Distributive factors relating to raw-materials*. -The distribution or marketing of raw materials such as extractive products and fabricating goods is also highly complicated by a number of important factors. The points of raw-material production are generally few and localized. The markets, too, are largely concentrated in industrial centers. Usually, raw materials are large in bulk as compared with their intrinsic value so that transportation costs are relatively of considerable importance. Storing and grading or sorting are necessary. Moreover, the wide variety of uses which the raw materials may be put involves reaching a large number of different markets. These uses are altered constantly by research and experimentation. The shadow of some possible substitute frequently clouds the whole marketing horizon. The volume of sale depends rather directly upon the rate of manufacturing activity. Wholesale and retail markets overlap because such raw materials as paint, textiles, and leather are sold for retail distribution as well as for industrial use. The principal middlemen engaged in marketing this group of products are: Commission merchants, brokers, sales agents, wholesalers, jobbers and retailers. Special types of middlemen like wholesale and retail dock and trestle coal companies and wholesale and retail dock and trestle coal companies and wholesale and retail lumber yard companies, independent or line (chain), are also common.

12. *Possibilities of using non-physical activities*. -The producer of raw materials and the raw-material middleman can make a much more intensive use of the non-physical marketing activities than can the farmer of the farm middleman. Market analysis for raw materials are

profitable because the exact needs of buyers can be determined rather accurately. The forecasting of supplies and price trends is important because raw materials are purchased on a price basis and very frequently on short or long-term contracts. Distribution policies can be worked out irrespective somewhat of traditional marketing channels. Definite policies on prices, such as guarantees against price declines, are possible. Equitable and fair policies towards consumers can be established to build up good will. Technically-trained salesmen can be employed, because raw material buyers are concentrated in industrial centers, do not require frequent visitation, and are glad to avail themselves of technical advice with respect to raw materials. Advertising may be employed effectively and economically particularly when it is directed toward the manufacturer. Ultimate consumer advertising is more costly and less productive of results. Although identification of raw materials by brands may be possible, most raw materials form component parts of finished products and the consumer is more likely to be interested in the brand of the finished product than in a raw-material brand on a part or element of the finished product.

13. *Technical or industrial commodities.* -Technical or industrial commodities are the equipment, tools and supplies used in manufacturing but not entering the finished product in its marketed form. These commodities are purchased for purely utilitarian purposes. They include such necessary goods as belting, tools, and office supplies and such installation goods as factory boilers, heavy cranes, and textile machinery. They are called technical commodities because technological considerations of design, quality and performance are the major determinates in their purchase and consequently in their manufacture.

14. *Distributive factors relating to technical commodities.* -Products for technical service present their special marketing problems. The total number of buyers is relatively small. Competition for markets is extremely keen. Market location has no inherent relationship to the distribution of population. The character of the market is determined by the particular use to be made of the product. Installation commodities, in particular, must fit the needs of the individual plant or industry. Buying on specification and to individual order is a common practice. Purchasing is carried on from the point of view of product performance. The buying test is the cost per unit of satisfactory service. Installation commodities are purchased at infrequent intervals and the unit of purchase is large. Accessory products are purchased more frequently but at irregular intervals and in varying amounts. Service obligations are imposed upon the seller, particularly in the case of installation equipment. The marketing functions are performed, in the main, by the manufacturer's representatives or sales agents, wholesalers or jobbers, and such special-type middlemen as mill-supply houses (wholesalers) and sales engineering concerns (sales agents). Certain kinds of accessory equipment such as wrenches, electrical supplies, automobile parts, bearings and fans, are handled also by retailers.

15. *Possibilities of using non-physical activities.* -Both the manufacturers of technical commodities and the middlemen handlers can make an effective use of several activities in scientific marketing procedure. Accurate and comprehensive market analyses are necessary to consummate initial orders, to secure repeat orders, and to avoid replacement by competitive products. Technical products are often purchased as the result of competitive bids and market

forecasting is absolutely essential to estimate production costs in terms of present and future raw material prices. Single distribution channels or mixed channels may be used as effectiveness and economy dictate. Technically-trained salesmen who competent to offer engineering advice may be employed with profitable results. Buyers begin to consider the purchase of installation equipment long before it is actually bought. They purchase necessary equipment irregularly and at very infrequent intervals. Hence advertising which is directed toward the industrial market and which stresses performance facts, design and construction details, exclusive advantages and service facilities will be most effective.

16. *Consumers' manufactured goods*. -consumers' manufactured goods are those fabricated products which are sold to the ultimate consumer-an individual or household. They may be classified on the basis of the characteristic purchasing behavior of the consumer. Thus, we have convenience goods, shopping goods, and specialties. The distinction is important. One major difficulty in the marketing of products has arisen from the tendency of the manufacturer, and even of the dealer, to think of their lines as staples. This conception, however, offers no key as to the correct marketing procedure to follow. It is essential to view products in the way the consumer looks at them.

Convenience goods are goods of small unit price in the purchase of which the consumer wishes to be put to a minimum of effort. Many of them come under the heading of so-called staple products. Groceries, tobacco, drugs, and similar items are typical examples. Neckties, collars, handkerchiefs, shirts, belts and other articles that are found usually on the counters just inside the doors of department stores are likewise convenience goods because they must be placed where the customer does not have to search for them. Shopping goods are those goods in the purchase of which the consumer desires to compare prices, qualities and styles. Chinaware, yard goods, clothing, jewelry, and so on, are typical shopping goods. Specialty goods are those which have some particular attraction for the consumer other than price alone. Their purchase is important and infrequent enough to induce the purchaser to visit a distant retail store, if necessary. A Hickey-Freeman suit, a Dunhill pipe, a Mark Cross briefcase, or an Electrolux refrigerator are examples of products which may be specialty goods as far as the individual consumer is concerned. The term "specialty" as applied to goods must not be confused with "specialty" as applied to stores. In connection with goods it implies high quality and a certain degree of exclusiveness, but in connection with stores it implies a limitation of the nature of products carried to types, such as groceries, or hardware, or clothing.

17. *Relative importance of physical and non-physical activities*. -Consumers' manufactured goods are produced in quantity for sale to wide markets. They are intensively marketed through middlemen and pass to the individual or the family usually through retail outlets. Broadly speaking, the problems of physical handling are somewhat less important in the distribution of consumers' manufactured goods than the problems of performing effectively and economically the several non-physical distributive activities.

However, this statement must not be extended in its meaning to belittle the importance of physical handling. It matters little that the market is well analyzed, the product line well chosen, the field sales campaign well planned, the advertisements well written and placed in mediums that pull-no amount of psychology or promotion will result in continuously profitable sales without an effective and economical physical handling of the goods from the maker to the consumer. With this word of caution, it should be said again that market research, market forecasting, the formulation of definite market policies, and careful planning for personal salesmanship and advertising are particularly essential to mass distribution. The manufacturer of consumers' goods and the middlemen who handle consumers' goods can make a more intensive and extensive use of these steps in scientific marketing procedure than can the producer or middleman engaging in distributing any other class or group of products. In spite of this fact, it is probable that more economic wastes exist in distributing consumers' goods than in any other field of distribution. And most of these wastes are the result of an ineffective and careless performance of the non-physical marketing activities or the failure to perform some of them at all.

18. *Services and intangible products.* -The final group of vendible "commodities" is composed of services and intangible products. The services which fall into this group may be personal and technical advice or the actual and personal execution of some definite commission. They may be the professional services of physicians, surgeons, dentists, clergymen, lawyers, engineers, and accountants, or the skilled labor service of the plumber and the carpenter. They may be the semi-professional services of the advertising agency or of the collection agency. They may be the non-professional services of the public utility. The "intangibles" may be bank credit, securities, insurance or statistical services. Obviously, this group of intangibles is exceedingly varied in the nature of its component elements.

19. *Distributive factors relating to services and intangible products.* -As a general rule, the distribution or marketing of services is not a highly organized process. Personal services are individualistic and consequently are marketed usually on a one-man basis. Few middlemen take a hand in the process. Occasionally the broker and the commission man become more important factors but, on the whole, personal services do not lend themselves to middleman handling. Personal services cannot be standardized and produced in quantity to any extent. Often they cannot be accurately described. They cannot be transported, classified and measured in the sense of physical products. Accordingly, sales are mainly direct and the functionaries of distribution are absent. In the case of intangibles like insurance and securities more elaborate marketing techniques are usually employed. Insurance may be sold by the insurance company's own sales organization or through middlemen known as insurance brokers. Securities may be marketed directly to individuals, stock brokerage houses or institutions by the issuing business enterprise or through such financial middlemen as the financial broker, the mortgage companies, the investment banking houses, the commercial paper houses, and the commercial credit companies, or through organized security exchanges. Ordinary bank credit, of course, is obviously a matter of direct exchange between a lender and a borrower.

20. *Effective use of marketing facilities.* -Such, then, are the principal groups of vendible commodities and their respective limitations or possibilities with respect to the use of several non-physical marketing activities. In this text, our discussion of marketing will be confined to the effective and economical use of these non-physical marketing activities. We will touch upon

the physical handling of goods only incidentally. This procedure will be followed for a number of reasons. In the first place, the function of *distribution* is all-inclusive but the function of *marketing* is concerned primarily with the non-physical problems of reaching the consumer. Gorton James, who formerly was Chief of the Domestic Commerce Division of the United States Department of Commerce, put the situation as follows: "We take 'distribution' to cover all the problems of getting goods from the producer to the consumer. Of course, these are the two phases-marketing and physical handling." In the second place, most of the criticism which is at present directed against the whole field of distribution is aimed at marketing in particular, at "frenzied" salesmanship and "prodigal" advertising. Finally, it appears that the possibilities of improving commodity distribution are greatest in connection with the effective and economical use of these true marketing functions. Certainly, the growing recognition of the value of staff marketing activities is opening way for study analysis which must inevitably produce beneficial results.

21. *Application to the field of consumers' goods.* -The discussion of the ways and means of using these non-physical distributive activities will be confined mainly to manufactured consumers' goods. This type of goods, as has been indicated, presents the greatest possibilities for an extensive and intensive application of the marketing function. It is in the process of reaching the consumer with manufactured goods that we now find actual examples and evidence of what can be accomplished by using these non-physical marketing techniques. Naturally, much that will be said in connection with market research, market forecasting, the formulation of definite market policies, and careful market planning can be and is frequently applied to the problem of distributing technical or industrial commodities, and even to the problems of distributing raw materials.

WHOLESALE MIDDLEMEN OF CONSUMER GOODS

1. *The function of the wholesale middleman.* -The wholesale middleman is the link between the manufacturer and the retailer. His purpose is to bring the one into contact with the other, either directly or indirectly, to facilitate the distribution of manufactured goods. He is not, as some erroneously believe, a newcomer or the result of twentieth century methods of mass-production. The middleman has been with us since the dawn of commerce. He performs a definite and necessary function in the field of selling. Retailers depend upon him to fill their orders. Manufacturers depend upon him to secure buyers for their products.

2. *How middlemen are classified.* -There are a number of ways in which manufacturers and retailers are kept in touch with each other. Consequently, middlemen are classified

according to the particular methods of contact which they employ. There are commission merchants, brokers, manufacturers' representatives or sales agents, and jobbers or wholesalers. These names are indicative of the type of work which the middlemen perform. There are, however, various sub-classifications. For instance, brokers are divided into three groups: Buying brokers, selling brokers, and merchandising brokers. Another classification can be set up according to the number and variety of products handled, that is, there are general and specialty jobbers.

The definition given below must not be too strictly construed. Business has little respect for dictionaries. Changes in local conditions often bring about corresponding changes in the functions which a middleman performs. They do not necessarily effect a change in the name of the service. Many middlemen are designated as brokers, yet they carry stocks of goods and bill in their own name. many who merely make collections for the manufacturer are listed as commission merchants. This rather loose use of terms need not cause confusion, because the terms are quite elastic. A commission merchant performs one type of service, a broker another, and a sales-agent still another. If a man who starts in business as a broker really becomes a commission merchant but prefers to call himself by his original designation, nothing can be done about it. It is enough for our purpose to say that the designation is a misnomer.

3. *The role of the commission merchant.* -A commission merchant is a middleman who receives consignments of merchandise from a principal, sells them and returns the proceeds of the sale to the owner, collecting for himself a commission. All of his business, however, is transacted in his own name, which heads his bill of sale. Prior to sale and delivery, he has actual possession of the goods in which he deals. Though bound to follow the instructions of the principal for whom he acts, he is allowed a certain amount of leeway in quoting prices and making terms. As a rule, all selling costs come out of his commission. Other expenses such as storage, handling and insurance of the goods while in his possession, are paid by the principal.

Some commission merchants prefer to operate under a system whereby they assume all expenses incurred from the point of shipment to the actual delivery of goods to the retailer. In these cases, the rate of commission is higher. It is higher, also, if the commission merchant guarantees collections on his sales. Rates of commission vary from trade to trade. In some lines the rate is as high as 10 per cent, in others as low as two percent. In those cases, where the principal pays all the expenses of handling, the rate is low, usually two to three per cent. It is, however, gross profit. The rate is necessarily high when the commission merchant has to pay these various costs himself.

4. *The role of the broker.* -A broker differs from a commission merchant in two respects. He does not possess the goods which he sells and he does not bill in his own name. His responsibilities do not extend to the handling or delivery of the goods. He may operate on his own account and may relay the order of a buyer to the principal who pays him the highest commission. If he limits his sales to the output of a single factory, as frequently happens, he is scarcely distinguishable from a sales agent. Because of his proximity to the market and his knowledge of supply and demand, a broker can frequently get very good prices for his principal. He may sell to jobbers as well as to retailers. He has nothing to do with collections. The

purchaser makes all payments to the principal unless special authority to receive payment has been given to the broker. Prices and terms of payment are likewise under the control of the principal.

A broker's operating expenses are usually very small. He does not require and office or even a desk room. He may divide his time between the office of his principal and the offices of his prospective customers. The telephone offers ample facility for most of his activities. He spends a large part of the day calling manufacturers and relaying the bids of his customers or calling customers and quoting the prices of manufacturers. His work is completed with the signing of the customer's order or the acceptance of the bid by the manufacturer. Cancellation of the order, on the other hand, may deprive the broker of his commission.

5. *Three types of brokers*. -Not all brokers do both buying and selling. Some specialize in buying, others in selling. Another class not only buys and sells but does a little merchandising as well. For this reason, we have to-day buying brokers, selling brokers, and merchandising brokers.

6. *Buying brokers*. -Buying brokers keep in close touch with market conditions at all times. Knowing where certain lines and grades of goods are to be found and the probable prices and terms, they can render valuable service to buyers. Their work consists in finding someone who has the amount and kind of goods desired and purchasing them for their principals. They are paid on a commission basis or by a flat rate per month or week of service.

7. *Selling brokers*. -Selling brokers, as their name indicates, limit their activities to the selling end of the brokerage business. They are kept informed of the amount and kind of goods that their employers have on hand and also what prices and terms are. With this information they seek buyers. Practically all selling brokers are paid on a commission basis. They may work for one manufacturer or for several in the same line of production.

8. *Merchandising brokers*. -In buying goods for jobbers and retailers, brokers who buy as well as sell often purchase some items on their own account. These items are stored until a buyer appears before them. It may be that there are a number of small retailers in a district who are frequently in need of small quantities of goods. The broker who buys small lots on his own account can keep these retailers supplied and make a substantial profit in so doing. It is sometimes considered good policy for a broker whose orders call for three-quarters of the space of a freight car to buy the other quarter for himself and dispose of the goods thus received to retailers in small lots. This purchase, storage and resale of goods is a function of merchandising rather than brokerage. The practitioners of this added function are called merchandising brokers.

A merchandising brokerage business can be conducted on a very profitable basis. By keeping in stock the goods which yield him the greatest return and filling part of his orders from this stock and relaying the other items to be filled by his principal, the merchandising broker can make a substantial income. The cost of operating his business is exceedingly low. A small portion of his profits he may pass on to his customers in the form of lower prices. In this respect he competes with the jobbers or wholesalers in the business and frequently brings condemnation on his head.

9. *The function of the manufacturer's representative.* -A manufacturer's representative or sales agent differs somewhat from a broker. He enters into a contract with the manufacturer in which the scope of his authority is specifically determined. His dealings with customers are binding on his principal as long as he acts within the scope of his agency. He has nothing to say about the prices but does have authority to promise deliveries and to extend credit.

These sales agents are divided into two classes. One group can be called traders. They maintain warehouses in which are stored complete stocks of manufacturer's goods. They have their own shipping services and send goods out as soon as orders are received. They bill the goods and undertake collection of the accounts. Agents of this type are necessary in certain lines. The grocery business, for instance, calls for shipments to retailers on short notice. A sales agent who has the goods on hand offers very attractive accommodation, and thereby increases his business.' The other group confines its activities to selling alone. These agents sell by sample and their orders are subject to the approval of their principal. They have nothing to do with delivery or collections. They are limited in territory also, being allowed to operate in a country, or a city, or even a section of a city. Like brokers and commission merchants, selling agents receive their compensation in the form of a commission.

Because of the diversity in the number and types of service which sales agents render to their principals the function of each individual agent cannot be defined here. One of them may represent as many as forty manufacturers. Of his forty contracts no two may be alike. They may call for a different type of service in each case. As a rule, a sales agent will give to a manufacturer whatever type of service the latter desires.

10. *The wholesaler or jobber.* - The last class of middlemen with which we will deal in this chapter is composed of the wholesalers or jobbers. In some sections of the country in certain lines of distribution there is a distinction drawn between the wholesale and the jobber. The term wholesaler is applied to those who buy usually in car-lots, the term jobber to those who may buy in less than car-lots. Quite often the jobber buys part of a carload from a wholesaler and sells it in still smaller lots to retailers. In Pittsburgh the market is a yard. Although Pittsburgh wholesales have store, they refer to the yard business as wholesale business and to store business as jobbing business. If any distinction is to be drawn between these two terms it is well to describe the wholesaler as one who sells most of his supplies to jobbers and other middlemen, and the jobber as one who supplies the retail merchants.

Jobbers or wholesalers are merchants. They deal on their own account. The goods which they buy from the manufacturer or producer they pay for whether they sell them or not. As owners of their own goods they can charge whatever they please, unless restricted by war-time regulations. Jobbers are classified in two ways: According to the number and variety of the products which they handle, and according to their adherence or departure from strictly jobbing functions.

11. *General and specialty jobbers.* -A general jobber is one who carries a complete line of merchandise. His goods may be hardware, groceries, boots and shoes, or drugs. He handles practically all items in these lines and can, if necessary, supply all the local stores with a

complete stock. The specialty jobber handles only a limited number of articles in each line, perhaps coffees and teas, or hosiery and gloves. If he is a specialty jobber in the hardware line his commodities may be only cutlery, or pots, pans, and other kitchen utensils. While the general shoe jobber handles anything from bedroom slippers to hunting boots, the specialty jobber may handle only ladies' dress shoes or men's work shoes.

It can readily be seen that the general jobber handles an innumerable variety of articles. A general jobber in the grocery line often carries ten thousand different items. In the boot and shoe business, if sizes are counted, the number may exceed fifty thousand. The specialty jobber who handles less than a hundred different items has far simpler problems to solve than the general jobber. However, there is not always a clear distinction between the general and the specialty jobber. The former may drop a large number of commodities from his lists and the latter may continually add to his. In these days of specialization, a dealer in cheese, specialized as that type of jobbing seems, is less a specialist than one who deals only in foreign-made cheese.

12. *True, semi-, and manufacturing jobbers.* -The second classification of jobbers, according to functions performed, divides them into three classes: (a) True jobbers, (b) semi-jobbers, and (c) manufacturing jobbers. The first we have already discussed. For the sake of clarity, it should be repeated here that a true jobber is one who buys in large quantities from a manufacturer and sells in small lots to a retailer.

13. *The development of the semi-jobber.* -A semi-jobber is a merchant who sells to both the wholesale and the retail trade. Very few start in business as semi-jobbers. Semi-jobbers are for the most part who began as retailers and have added wholesaling to their original function. They are numerous in the hardware business. In the clothing business their number is growing daily. In this line, however, the average semi-jobber was originally a true jobber who added retailing to his wholesale business.

The rise of the semi-jobber can be attributed to many causes. There is, first of all, the opportunity for a double profit. The added expense of operating a retail department is covered amply by the retail profit. Such a department serves also as an outlet for odd and broken lots of stock. In addition, it keeps the jobber in close contact with the ultimate consumer. His buying and selling can be done on a much sounder basis if he knows from day to day the attitude of the consumer. If the merchant has become a semi-jobber through the addition of a wholesale department to his already established retail department the incentive has been different. To secure the best prices from a manufacturer he has to buy in large quantities, or get his name on the jobbers list. A limited number of retail sales preluded his buying in large quantities, so he added to his list of customers the small shopkeepers in his neighborhood. In this way he was able to dispose of surplus stocks. His name appeared on the jobbers' list and he received the benefit of large discounts.

14. *The rise of the manufacturing jobber.* -We have seen that the effort to combine wholesale and retail trading resulted in the advent of the semi-jobber. A similar combination, that of manufacturing and jobbing, is responsible for the existence of the manufacturing jobber.

He is, in general, a jobber who does some manufacturing on his own account. Many of the candy, clothing, grocery, drug and jewelry jobbers have added the manufacturing feature to their wholesaling. In important distribution centers there are usually a large number of manufacturing jobbers. In the Cleveland area at least 80 per cent of the drug jobbers handle some goods which they manufacture especially for themselves. In New York probably 50 per cent of the jewelry jobbers may be termed manufacturing wholesalers.

The combination of these two functions has many advantages. Close contact with the ultimate source of supply results in economy of operation. Goods are prepared for shipment only when ordered. At other times they are stored in bulk. Another advantage is that the manufacturing jobber is not forced to secure an outlet for his goods. He manufactures only as much as he can dispose of to his customers. Jobbers who have their private brands can be assured of uniform quality of goods through their control of the manufacturing processes. Most important of all, the combination entitles the manufacturing jobber to two profits.

15. *The value of the middleman.* -Wholesale middlemen have been the subject of much criticism. The lay man, unfamiliar with methods of distribution, is prone to regard commission merchants, brokers, and jobbers as unnecessary units between the producer and the ultimate consumer, and their profits as one of the principal reasons for the high cost of commodities. A careful survey of modern business methods will prove the facts to be otherwise. Middlemen do make profits. But in return their profits they render valuable service to both manufacturers and retailers. The efficient operation of a wholesale business generally results in bringing commodities to the retailer at a price lower than when they are sold to him directly by the manufacturer.

16. *How the wholesaler serves the manufacturer.* -The services which the wholesaler renders to the manufacturer are numerous. In the first place, the wholesaler is a specialist and hence perform services for the manufacturer more cheaply than the latter can perform them for himself. The wholesaler knows what styles are most in demand, what quality of goods will be purchased, what sizes should be made in large quantities, and how large a volume can be sold. His knowledge extends even to the type of package that will be most suitable and attractive. Without this aid, the manufacturer would be compelled to make a detailed periodic study of market conditions. This trouble and expense is saved for him by the middleman.

17. *Providing steady customers.* -Through the wholesaler the manufacturer is provided with a clientele of steady customers whose patronage the dealer has solicited. The wholesaler's catalog is a form of advertising from which the manufacturer profits. Few manufacturers can handle the small orders of retailers as economically as the wholesaler. A hardware storekeeper, for example, may need fifty dollars' worth of goods the original source of which may be a dozen different factories scattered all over the country. A wholesaler can fill the entire bill from stock, ship the goods, and still make a profit. The individual manufacturers of the goods could not handle the separate two-dollar or three-dollar orders involved and cover the cost of shipment without incurring a loss.

In the United States there are over 100,000 towns and villages with a population of less than 1,000. Manufacturers cannot canvass these towns for orders. The wholesaler, on the other hand, can cover these districts intensively. Small as the orders are, a sufficient number of them will assure him of profits. In this respect the wholesaler renders important service to the manufacturer. He does his soliciting for him.

18. *Transportation and storage savings*. -Because he purchases his goods in large quantities the wholesaler saves the manufacturer large amounts in the cost of transportation, and in packing, shipping, accounting, and mailing departments of his business. Collection is made easier. It is less difficult to handle the accounts of 1,000 wholesalers than those of 100,000 retailers.

By providing storage for the manufacturer's goods the wholesaler renders indispensable service. Factories cannot be operated efficiency or economically under a succession of rush and slack periods. Yet these would occur if wholesalers did not purchase regularly in fairly large amounts. Otherwise, to even up the production schedule and at the same time maintain stocks of goods, the manufacturers would have to establish storage houses in different parts of the country. Such storage houses would entail a great expense which is saved to the manufacturer by the wholesaler.

19. *Wholesalers give manufacturers financial assistance*. -Manufacturers are often in need of financial assistance. Such assistance is at times given by the wholesaler who advances funds and accepts in return the contract for future delivery of goods which he needs. This is a common practice in the canning industry. The wholesaler extends a loan at the beginning of the production season. He is repaid in canned fruits and vegetables four or six months later. The wholesaler may also render indirect financial aid to the manufacturer. He may pay his bills promptly in an effort to get a cash discount.

The most important indirect method of financial assistance given by the wholesaler to the manufacturer is often overlooked-that of carrying the accounts of retail dealers. In the grocery business, for example, as much money is tied up in accounts receivable as in merchandise. In other lines these uncollected items vary in amount, often running as high as 30 to 50 per cent of the value of the merchandise. The amount of money saved to the manufacturer in this way is considerable.

20. *How the wholesaler serves the retailer*. -One of the principal functions of the wholesaler is assembling. The thousands of articles which he handles come from hundreds of factories in different parts of the country-sometimes even from abroad. He stores these products in his warehouses and sells them to retailers when they are wanted. The value of this service can be realized if we consider the number of manufacturers whose goods find their way into some

one retail store. In the United States there are hundreds of manufacturers of food products and hundreds of manufacturers of drugs. A retail grocer carrying in stock as many as 2,000 items, can purchase them all from three or four wholesalers. If he purchased directly from the manufacturer he would probably have to make out 1,500 different orders. The drug store with its stock of 10,000 items is a more striking example. All of these items can be purchased from two or three wholesalers, for the average drug jobber carries 50,000 different items in stock.

The wholesaler also offers buying facilities. His large stock, usually stored in one building, gives the retailer the opportunity of choosing from thousands of items. No factory or group of factories offers such accommodation. The wholesaler's catalog with its pictures, descriptions and prices of stock, also facilitate buying for the retailer.

21. *Wholesale economies are retail benefits*. -Quantity purchasing always entails low prices. The wholesaler buys in car-lots, thus obtaining his goods at a discount and saving in freight rates. Economies of this nature are usually passed on to the retailer. The ability to buy in small amounts and yet at a reasonably low prices is an advantage for which the retailer must thank the wholesaler.

The small merchant who carries a large number of items can operate at a profit only if he has a quick turnover of stocks. Frequent purchasing in small quantities would be an impossibility if the wholesaler did not exist. Usually factories fill only large orders and the small retailer's capital would be tied up in large quantities of few commodities. Were these conditions to prevail many retailers could not stay in business.

22. *Credit extended to retailers*. -Many retailers have been able to start in business because of the credit extended to them by the wholesalers. Many, already in business, would be forced to suspend operations if wholesalers were unwilling to grant long-term credit. The policy of wholesalers has always been to render whatever financial aid they possibly can to the honest and efficient retailer. This the manufacturer is unable to do because he is so far removed from the retailer that he is not acquainted with his credit standing. The wholesaler, on the other hand, operating within a limited territory, knows intimately almost every one of his customers. In the rare cases of uncertainty, he can very easily ascertain the reliability of any particular individual or company.

23. *The wholesaler a market adviser*. -The average retailer does not always know how rapidly certain commodities will sell. He is in doubt as to what items he should place on his stock. Valuable advice is often given on this point by the wholesaler. Through his numerous contacts with hundreds of other retailers the wholesaler knows what goods are most in demand. In fact, he can keep a well-balanced stock on the shelves of his retail customers. The salesmen of wholesale houses are often specialists in their fields. Realizing that the success of their ow concerns depends upon the success or the retailer consumers, they naturally endeavor to give advice that will be to the best interest of the retailers.

24. *Services of the broker*. -The broker is limited in the services he can render because of the narrower scope of his activities. The buying broker can relieve the manufacturer periodically of his stock and at the same time serve the retailers by purchasing for them quantities of goods

about which otherwise they might have no knowledge. He can also apprise them of special bargains existing in the producing field with which he maintains and intimate acquaintanceship. For example, manufacturers sometimes sell their products at a very low figure to acquire ready cash. The broker by acquainting his clients with this fact gives them an opportunity to take advantage of bargains.

The selling-broker's services are also two-fold. He aids the manufacturer by placing him in close contact with the people who wish to buy his goods. He aids the retailer by informing him of what manufacturers have to sell, and what the prices and terms will be. The merchandising broker adds one more kind of service. Through the maintenance of stock on his own account he can fill the orders of small retailers with whom manufacturers cannot deal at a profit.

25. *The services of the manufacturer's representative.* -The manufacturer who sells through representatives or sales agents has the advantage usually of a live, aggressive representative in the important centers of business. Operating, as they do, on a commission basis, the sales agents are paid only for the number of sales which they make. In an arrangement of this type there is no overhead, hence the manufacturer saves money. He also avoids the expense of maintaining district offices. Because the sales agent has an office in the local community the retailer is saved the trouble of going to a distant point to look at samples and to place his orders. Usually the sales agent carries samples of all the goods he sells. The knowledge that from these samples he can select and order goods in any desired quantity and at definite prices and terms of credit means much to the retailer.

26. *Commission merchants add further services.* -Commission merchants add still other services. Like the jobbers they store goods and thus relieve the manufacturer of the necessity of maintaining huge warehouses. In those cases, in which they make collections they save the manufacturer the cost of maintaining a collection department. The commission merchant's knowledge of the market gives him the opportunity to make better business deals than his principal could make.

The commission merchant's service to retailers includes all the services which the ordinary brokers and sales agents give plus the possession of stock from which ready deliveries can be made. In addition, a commission merchant finds it profitable to fill small orders. Retailers are thus enabled to buy in small quantities goods which they cannot purchase directly from the manufacturer.

RETAIL MIDDLEMEN OF CONSUMERS' GOODS

1. *Types of retail middlemen.* -Retail distribution is carried on by six types of merchandising establishments. These are the general store, the specialty store, which may be a neighborhood store or a downtown shop, the department store, the chain store, the mail-order house, and the cooperative store. The last-named type is not an important retail outlet in this country. These types differ from each other in the number and variety of commodities that they sell, in their methods of distribution, and in their system of management.

2. *The general store.* -The first and probably the oldest types is the general store. Located chiefly in small towns and villages, it serves the entire community with all that it needs-groceries, hats, shoes, suits, dry goods, and hardware. In spite of the diversity of articles it carries the purchaser has little or no variety from which to choose. The general store, in most cases, has only one or two makes of shoes, only one or two brands of canned goods, and similarly limited selections in other lines. It is owned and operated, as a rule, by some individual who becomes well-known throughout the town or village.

The general store will continue to be a necessity in many communities for years to come. The volume of business transacted in any one particular line is not sufficient to warrant the establishment of separate neighborhood grocery stores, hardware stores, and clothing stores. There are about 150,000 general stores scattered throughout the towns and villages of the United States.

3. *Why the general store is being displaced.* -When a town grows in population the prosperity of the general store begins to wane. The quantities of groceries, shoes, and cloths which are purchased are sufficient to warrant the opening of separate stores each carrying one or a few of these lines. These stores usually outsell the general store because of the variety of their stock. A shoe store, for instance, gives the purchaser the opportunity of choosing between many different lines, whereas the general store offers him merely two or three. Under competition of this type the general store naturally loses customers.

Other factors responsible for the disappearance of general stores from small communities are the improvements that have come about in the means of highway transportation and communication. The townsmen or villagers who own automobiles prefer to shop in the larger stores of the nearby cities. With the extension of the telephone system and the unusual accommodations offered by the city stores, the residents of small communities can have delivered in one day's time at their doors the groceries, hardware, and dry goods which they order by telephone from the stores of the city. Other channels of distribution sech as the mail-order houses have also weakened the position of the general store.

4. *Advantages of the general store.* -In spite of the strong competition of mail-order houses and the larger stores of the neighboring cities general stores held a surprisingly large amount of their trade.

It is, after all, more convenient to shop in the neighborhood store than one located twenty miles away. In case of difficulties or errors adjustments can be made almost immediately. Delivery is quicker and credit is usually extended. The bulk of the townspeople purchase in small quantities and only as they need commodities. In the matter of groceries, they buy each day what they expect to consume that day. They do not anticipate their wants to the extent of making distant city shopping practicable. They also know the general storekeeper personally. Each trip is somewhat in the mature of a visit and tends to cement the bonds between buyer and seller. Through his personal knowledge of his customers' desires the general store owner knows just what stock to keep.

The general store enjoys a number of minor advantages. Rents are low, salaries are small, and operating expenses, as a rule, amount too little. Intimate knowledge of his customer's resources enables the owner to avoid credit losses. Thriving as it usually does on the sale of convenience goods, that is, goods which supply ordinary everyday needs, the general store is assured o steady patronage. No advertising is necessary beyond the personal solicitation which takes place in the store. In a small village there is no distinction between potential and real customers; all are real customers.

5. *Some disadvantages of the general store.* -There are some very definite disadvantages attached to the operation of a general store. One of these, already mentioned, is the limited volume and variety of merchandise offered for the customer's selection. The slow and irregular sale of some goods results in shop-worn merchandise. Goods once popular are left on the shelves because of the changing styles and demands. The owner must of necessity buy in small quantities and thus pays a higher price for his goods. Buying as he does to satisfy a wide range of human desires, he cannot become a specialist in any one field. The greatest disadvantage of all, however, lies in inefficiency of management. Years of trade without active competition is the factor probably responsible for this inefficiency.

6. *The specialty store.* -The second type of retail outlet is the specialty store. This is a single retail unit which handles a limited amount of merchandise. In speaking of the specialty store we refer to the kinds of lines handles and not their quality. Popular phraseology has adapted the term "specialty" to apply to types of goods which are "exclusive" and high-priced. By a specialty store, however, we mean one which limits its stocks to certain definite kinds of products. One store will limit itself to girdles, underwear, and stockings, another to haberdashery, a third to groceries, a fourth to hardware, and a fifth to drugs.

Two types of specialty stores now in existence are known as neighborhood stores, and downtown, or exclusive stores. Location determines the classification and the difference in stock. The neighborhood store serves the community in which it is located. People buy from it because they live in the neighborhood. The downtown type does not necessarily serve the residents of the district in which it is located.

The neighborhood specialty stores carry both convenience and shopping goods. A men's hat store in some local section of any one of our large cities is a typical example. The hats are shopping goods. The downtown specialty store is often exclusive in its stock. In every city there are several such stores which carry lines of specialty goods that can be purchased nowhere else.

7. *The neighborhood specialty store.* -If the specialty store is a neighborhood store it enjoys other advantages. It is more convenient than the downtown department store. Its customers are residents of the neighborhood and therefore rather regular in their patronage. By exercising care in the selection of his stock, the proprietor may outdo the downtown department stores in the variety and attractiveness, if not in the volume, of his commodities.

The chief disadvantage which the neighborhood specialty store owner has to face lies in buying. Purchasing as he does in small quantities he pays a rather high wholesale rate for his goods. Nor does he purchase enough to warrant the services of a special buyer. In this respect the chain stores have a decided advantage over him. Lack of competition in his own neighborhood does not always work to the specialty store owner's benefit. At best he can get only the patronage of the neighborhood. Some of this patronage he has to sacrifice because confirmed shoppers prefer to go to the downtown districts where they can compare prices, travel from store to store, and see what bargains are being offered. Advertising is not as a rule feasible for the neighborhood specialty store. Posters, handbills, or window displays are probably the only practical mediums. A newspaper advertisement would be of no interest to ninety per cent of the people whom it might reach. The ten per cent who constitute a particular specialty store's patronage would be interested, but the cost of reaching such a limited group in this way would be too expensive. The chain stores have had an advantage over the specialty store in this respect. Their large scale advertising is warranted by the existence of at least one store in each neighborhood.

8. *The downtown or exclusive specialty store.* -The downtown specialty store has one definite advantage over the neighborhood store. If it is located in the general shopping district it attracts the attention of all the people who patronize the department stores. Because of its rather low overhead expenses, its wide variety of goods, and its personal service feature, the downtown specialty shop may compete very favorably with the department stores for the trade of these people.

Men, as a class, do not like department stores. They prefer to do their buying in small shops. The large crowds, the lack of personal interest, and the amount of effort required to locate certain departments deter them from entering the department stores. Shopping in the specialty store is quicker and more comfortable. Tis accounts, in a great measure, for the business success of men's shops in the downtown districts.

The highly specialized stores locate in the downtown districts for many reasons. In the first place, they are convenient to a large number of prospective purchasers. They do not suffer unduly the competition of the department stores for they carry quality or kinds of goods which the department stores do not stock. This exclusiveness of stock gives them a monopoly in certain restricted lines. They can afford to advertise on a large scale because their patrons come from all points in the city.

9. *Large-scale retailing.* -Many factors have been responsible for the development of large-scale retailing in America. Increased prosperity, the improvement in highways, the extension of railroad lines, the institution of the parcel post system, and the spread of telephones are probably the most important of these factors. The availability of capital makes large ventures possible. The possession of money makes people a bit more fastidious in satisfying their desires. The newspapers with their Sunday supplements acquaint them with the latest styles. Railroads, motor tucks and the parcel post system make distant deliveries economically possible. Telephones facilitate ordering from the neighboring city.

Mail-order houses, chain-store systems, and department stores now do a large part of the retail business of the country. Some of these organizations now number their customers by the hundred thousand. Their activities are nation-wide. They purchase goods in enormous quantities. Some of them have their own manufacturing plants. All in all, they constitute the greatest retail systems of distribution the world has ever known. Because of the difference in their methods of operation they must be given individual consideration.

10. *The department stores as a retail outlet.* -After mail-order houses and chain-store systems, department stores are the next largest of all retail outlets. A department store is a retail establishment organized to consolidate the ownership, management and sale of many lines of merchandise under one roof. The goods it sells are divided into classes, each one of which is handled as a department, distinct as to management and location within the store, and carried on the accounts as a separate entity. Normally, dry goods constitute one of the most important departments. The number of departments may vary from a dozen to a hundred or more.

11. *Types of department stores.* -There are wide differences between department stores. Many, with their furniture, clothing, grocery, jewelry, toilet accessory, drug, toy, and other departments, are able to supply all the needs of the family. Others have a tendency to specialize. Their stock is limited to dry goods, clothing, hats, shoes, and similar lines. Some, while they operate many departments, exploit one department more than the others. In one store it may be furniture, in another men's clothing and in another women's wear.

12. *Advantages of the department store.* -As a rule, department stores are centrally located. S hopping goods constitute the majority of their sales. They are primarily women's stores. With women doing about eighty-five per cent of all the purchasing in America it is not surprising that the department stores and mail-order houses together do about ten per cent of all the retail business. The appeal of the department store lies partly in the convenience of doing all of one's shopping under one roof. The larger stores have another appeal; each one of their departments carries a wider variety of goods than the specialty store engaged in the same line.

From the standpoint of management and ownership department stores may be divided into three classes: first, those stores in which all of the departments are owned and controlled by a single central organization.; second, the type in which the so-called owners of the store own merely the building and rent space to a number of independent units, each unit paying the rent for its space and an additional amount for services such as delivery, the maintenance of information booths, and floor-walker's supervision; third, and most numerous, those stores in which a majority of the departments are owned and operated by one central organization, with a few departments leased to independent units.

13. *Department store savings and services.* -The department store enjoys all the advantages common to large retail units, and several in addition. It has a system of accounting whereby the profit and loss record of each department is closely checked. This system enables the owners to increase general profits by discontinuing those goods or those departments that are unable to pay an adequate return. because these stores usually are centrally located they derive full benefit from large-scale advertising. One of their chief advantages lies in the act that purchasers in going to the particular counters that they seek pass through numerous other departments that attract their attention and solicit heir custom. The facility of buying all kinds of articles in one building is another attractive feature. In its appeal to the family the department store offers many inducements to the woman with children. Playrooms under the supervision of a nurse are provided in which children can be left while their parents shop. Restaurants prelude the necessity of interrupting shopping by going elsewhere for lunch. Waiting rooms make convenient meeting places and offer facilities for rest. Some stores go so far as to provide free concerts and entertainments. A few have rather attractive art galleries. Fashion- shows are held periodically in many. Services of this nature give the department store a decided advantage over its competitors.

Department stores buy in large quantities and thus gain the advantage of reduced costs on their goods. Many of their articles are purchased directly from the manufacturer, and thus the jobbers' profit is saved. Bu means of its centralized shipping room and delivery system the department store is able to send to the homes of its customers in one lot the articles purchased from many different departments. This is an economy. The privilege of returning goods is extended by all department stores. They also extend credit to a greater degree than any of the competing types of stores. The amount of business transacted warrants the employment of efficient supervisors, merchandising specialists, accountants, credit men, and advertising agents.

14. *Disadvantages of department-store operation.* -The disadvantages of department-store operation are nevertheless numerous. Much of the attractive service is abused. Large amounts of goods are returned because the purchaser finds a better bargain in another department store or specialty shop, or because the returned goods have been purchased merely on approval.

15. *Department store vs. specialty store.* -The employment of a large number of workers brings many problems in its wake. The service may become impersonal. Certain employees may lack interest in making sales, and sometimes disregard the policies of the store. Without special training many department store employees many department store employees are incapable of dealing with the numerous types of people constituting the patronage. In some cases, it takes almost a specialist to cater to the needs of the shopper. In this respect the specialty shop has a decided advantage over the department store. It is difficult for the department store to secure and hold the trade of the wealthier classes. Such people prefer the less crowded

establishment, the more exclusive class of goods and the numerous personal attentions offered by the specialty store.

Advertising costs are a large item of expense in a department store. Space must be bought in all the leading newspapers and in a large metropolitan area advertising also has to be carried in the newspapers of neighboring towns. The distribution of advertising material by mail to thousands or hundreds of thousands of prospective customers is another costly item. General overhead expenses are, of course, very high. Department stores are located in shopping districts where real estate valuations, and consequently property investments or rent, are high. All the services that must be provided are costly in themselves and cut down the profits of the business. The average department store department store in America today spends for operating expenses between 25 and 30 per cent of its total receipts from sales.

16. *Chain stores as retail outlets.* -among the large retail outlets in America is the chain-store system, which has accounted for about one-third of total retail volume annually. Up to the imposition of chain-store taxes by the various states and the enactment of the Robinson-Patman Act in 1936 and the state fair-trade laws made nationally effective by the Miller-Tydings Act of 1937 (all of which will be discussed later), chain stores bade fair to outstrip all competitors in retail distribution.

A chain store is one unit of a large group of retail establishments handling practically the same line of merchandise and operating under single ownership and management. The chain may be limited geographically to the cities and towns of a country or a state. Some chains are nation-wide; they have stores all the way from New York to San Francisco.

17. *Chain store not a distinct type.* -The chain store is not a distinct type of store. There may be chains of grocery stores such as the Great Atlantic and Pacific Tea Company, or general stores such as the J.C. Penney Stores, or drug stores such as the Liggett Drug Company, or department stores such as the Hahn Department Stores, or specialty stores of the neighborhood variety such as Young's Hat Stores, or exclusive shops such as Knox's. Chains are more numerous in the cities and large towns than in less urbanized localities.

18. *Advantages of the chain store.* -The growth of chain stores up to 1936 is easily explainable. Their organization and system of merchandising make possible low prices and reasonable profits. They buy in enormous quantities, and as a rule, directly from the manufacturer, which saves them a large amount of money. Their strong financial backing enables them to acquire the most desirable locations for their stores. They have advertising, sales and merchandising specialists who study markets, locations and community factors.

In competition with independent stores, the chains have had many advantages. With their large-scale advertising, they reach all their potential customers. A chain's established reputation is a form of advertising in itself. The presence of the name of the chain on a store window indicates immediately to all passers-by the type of goods sold and the relative prices charged. The prices are often lower than those of the independent stores, a most decided advantage in retail trade, made possible by the general efficiency of management and the low prices paid for goods purchased in large quantities. Chain stores can make experiments which the independent shopkeeper would not dare to make. They can test the selling appeal of certain articles in one store and apply the same results to all of their stores located in the same type of community.

19. *The low cost of chain-store operation.* -The chain store usually extends no credit and provides, with some exceptions, no delivery service. The entire business is operated primarily on a cash-and-carry basis. Costs of delivery and losses from bad debts are thereby avoided or reduced. If the business is conducted on a self-service basis, as in the Piggly Wiggly stores, clerks' salaries are also eliminated. All of these factors are responsible for the low cost of operation. The average grocery chain store of America spends 10 per cent pf its total income on operation, while the independent grocery merchant spends between 14 and 16 per cent.

20. *Difficulties of chain-store operation.* -In addition to punitive legislation, however, he difficulties of chain-store operations are numerous. The managers of the various stores have not the personal contact with the customers that independent storekeepers usually have, nor are they as vitally interested in the success of the business. Some chains attempt to overcome this difficultly by the manager a share of the profits of the chain. Separated by thousands of miles from the central office of control, however, the store managers tend to get out of contact with the policies of the chain. Patronage is also sacrificed through the local manager's inability to contribute to local charities, advertise in school programs, and join in town and city celebrations. A cash business likewise has certain drawbacks. There will probably always be a large class of customers to whom credit is a necessity. Various efforts, of course, are made to overcome these disadvantages.

Supermarkets, originally set up to compete with chain stores, have to some extent helped to solve the legislative difficulties facing the chains. Supermarkets and chain stores are alike that both apply the principles of mass selling. Chain stores make small profits from many customers reached through a large number of small neighborhood stores. The supermarket draws customers from a wider area to one store and there gives them benefits of mass buying and selling.

21. *The mail-order house as a retail outlet.* -A mail-order house is a retail distributing institution which makes sales and deliveries by mail instead of through personal contact. Mail-order houses may be divided roughly into four classes. Some, like Sears, Roebuck and Company and Montgomery Ward and Company are general and also operate a chain of retail stores. They carry in stock and sell a large variety if every class of goods needed in the home for personal use, toys, drugs, stationery, certain types of small equipment and farm implements, and numerous other lines. They also sell ready-cut lumber for building complete homes, and all the heating, plumbing and lighting equipment and fixtures required. Many of these items they make or have manufactured especially for their trade. Another class consists of those houses which carry one line, such as cloaks or suits, hardware, automobile tires, or jewelry. The third class consists of manufacturers who sell their products by mail directly to the consumer. Those in the fourth class are not strictly mail-order houses; they are rather department stores which do a mail-order business along with their usual store business.

22. *Methods of mail-order distribution.* -With the exception of the fourth class listed above, practically all mail-order houses have an unlimited area of distribution. The very largest ones do a nationwide business. The smaller concerns may limit active operations to two or three states but usually they, too, will fill orders from any part of the country. The majority of the mail-order house patrons live in small towns or villages. All mail-order houses send out catalogs containing pictures, descriptions and prices of their stocks. As a rule, the customer pays the mail, express and freight charges, although some larger houses are now prepaying shipments.

A highly specialized organization is necessary for the operation of a mail-order house. Careful descriptions of articles must be written up and the appeal value of these descriptions tested. Catalogs must be distributed to those who are interested in the company's goods. An efficient order-filling system is required to avoid errors that are both inconvenient to the customer and costly to the company. The order-assembly and shipping departments must always be prompt in dispatching articles. Mail-order purchasing of necessity causes the customer to wait at least two or three days for the receipt of the goods, and avoidable delay cannot be tolerated. Huge stocks must be maintained. Thousands of items, many in dozen different sizes, must be available at all times. Some mail-order houses, however, obviate the necessity if carrying large stocks by shipping some of their goods directly from the manufacturer to the purchaser. Mail-order houses that maintain their own factories also follow this method of distribution.

23. *Advantages of mail-order distribution.* -Their complete and varied lines of merchandise give the mail-order houses a decided advantage in competing with small town stores. The price charged by mail-order houses are lower, as a rule, than those of the rural stores. The styles carried are more in demand because they are looked upon as city styles. In competition with the department stores of a neighboring city the mail-order houses have the advantage that it is easier to buy by mail than it is to travel to the city.

Certain operating expenses of a mail-order house are comparatively low. The buildings are mainly warehouses. They can be located in that part of the city where real estate values are lowest. The cost of expensive fixtures is eliminated. The catalog and the reputation of the company are its real sales agents so that no retail sales force is necessary. The employees are mainly shippers and clerks. Most of the business is done on a cash basis and there is no necessity for a large credit department.

24. *Some handicaps of the mail-order system.* -There are many people who will not buy goods unless they actually see them. This is especially true in regard to clothing. The patronage of this class the mail-order houses cannot acquire. Others object to the delays incurred in mail-order buying. The prevalent tendency to patronize home or neighborhood stores also cuts into the business of the mail-order houses. As already pointed out, the extension of credit by general, specialty and department stores draws trade. Mail-order houses are not now and probably never will be in a position to extend much credit to buyers, except on goods of high unit value sold on the installment plan.

To overcome some of these difficulties mail-order houses are adding to their display and distribution systems by opening retail stores in the large cities. These stores are not located in the shopping districts and hence they attract as new customers mainly that class of people who merely hesitated to buy without seeing an article of purchase. The innovation has been very successful, and has accounted for as much as 60 per cent of the total annual business of companies adopting the plan.

25. *The consumers' cooperative stores.* -A cooperative store is one in which the stock is owned by the consumers. It is operated primarily for the purpose of buying in quantity and relaying he money thus saved to the consumer in the form of low prices. The originators of the idea felt that goods were high because of the profits exacted by middlemen. The establishment of cooperative associations eliminated one class, the retail storekeeper. In his place there appeared the store manager, an employee of the "association." Cooperative stores are not so popular in America as in England and on the continent; they constitute a relatively unimportant retail outlet in the United States.

26. *Why cooperative stores do not thrive in America.* -The numerous failures of "cooperatives" in the United States can be traced to several causes. American people move so often from city to city, town to city, and state to state that membership is continually changing. In addition, they are unwilling to subject themselves to the inconvenience of shopping in the cooperative store. The little money saved thereby is not so important to the average American as to the European. Moreover, American cooperative stores, for some reason or other, have not been fortunate in engaging good managers.

However, the cooperative societies have not disappeared entirely from America and probably never will. There are a number of them in the middle and western part of the country and many of them are successful. In some cases, they have decided advantages in their favor. Quantity purchasing saves them considerable money. Located on side streets as they usually are, they pay low rents. They have no advertising expense and need no special salesmen. Clerks can serve the needs of all the customers, for sales are not pushed. The patrons buy merely what they wish. As a rule, there are no delivery expenses. If the stores do business on a cash basis bad debts are eliminated, more favorable prices are secured in purchasing from wholesalers because of the ready cash, and a complicated bookkeeping system is rendered unnecessary. The absence of profit also reduces prices.

Cooperative have always been more popular in farm areas. During the last few years, however, forces favoring the cooperative idea have renewed their efforts to push the development of this type of store units or groups.

Lecture Two

MARKET RESEARCH-THE MARKET

1. *Importance of study of the market*. -Market policies which may be projected for any considerable period cannot be sound and successful if formulated on guesses and hunches. Marketing campaigns will inevitably be wasteful unless they are based definitely on precise methods of analysis of market data. The market is the objective of production and it must be defined, classified, evaluated, interpreted and measures before goods are manufactured. Product research is conducted in the light of the market. Competition, likewise, must be studied in connection with the possibilities of the general market.

2. *Definition of the market*. -The term "market" often is defined as a collection of individual consumers who are able, willing, and ready to buy a given product. In this sense, the individual manufacturer, or distributor uses the word "market" possessively and with either a present or future significance. Such a definition, of course, is quite different from the more impersonal and economic meaning of "a place or area where the rights to goods are bought and sold, and toward which and from which are the actual goods tend to travel." In our discussion we shall adhere to the business meaning. Manifestly, the producer's or manufacturer's market is usually divided into two parts: (a) immediate customers-the wholesalers and retailers to whom he sells, and (b) the ultimate market- the individual consumers for whom his products are produced or manufactured. Because the ultimate market is the essential guide to business activity, and the immediate market unquestionably depends upon the ultimate market, the ultimate market will be chiefly considered in this chapter.

3. The two types of market data. -The market, in the sense of collective consumers, must not be considered exclusively as an abstract, inanimate, and impersonal consuming force. Although the "market" may connote economic tendencies, the distribution of population, and

other factors, it concerns mainly the highly personal and animate individual consumer and his buying motives and habits. The study of the "market" may be statistical, but the stimulation of the individual consumer's willingness to buy is fundamental to sales. And the approach to the individual is largely psychological. Thus, any survey of market facts quite definitely involves two kinds of data, (a) quantitative and (b) qualitative. Each type has a definite significance and when classified and interpreted correctly will suggest essential marketing policies and effective and economical methods for market campaigns.

4. *Principal market factors*. -The most important "market" factors that should be surveyed are:

   (a) The territorial extent of the market

   (b) The character of the market

   (c) The potentialities of the market

   (d) The limitations on the market

   (e) The status of competition

   (f) Qualitative market factors such as age, sex, race, religion, occupation, class, operating knowledge, amusements and recreations, prejudices, buying habits, buying motives and buying capacity

While these factors apply chiefly to the problems of the manufacturer, many of them are equally applicable to the wholesaler, and some, at least, are of value to the retailer.

5. *Extent of the market*. -It is important first to classify the market on the basis of its territorial extent. Markets may be local. They may be limited to the community in which the producer or dealer is located. Such a market is reached quickly and at low cost. Sometimes the market is local because of a factor such as transportation which definitely marks out a natural area. Markets may also be state-wide, sectional, national, or international. Whatever the extent may be, one question must be considered fully and careful market analysis will disclose its answer: Is the market to be covered a natural market? Political boundary lines in most cases do not define a market. When the manufacturer of sewing machines, or typewriters, or automobiles, considers this question, because of the nature of these products, he can probably answer with the statement that his is a national or world market. When the manufacturer of cement considers his market, he must also ask: Where does the matter of freight rates begin to operate in favor of my competitors? The answer to this question sets up the limit of his market. If the manufacturer has some monopoly control over the supply of his product as the result of a patent or copyright, or controls the source of the supply, his market comprises every one who is likely to consume his product. If the product is one that can be produced just as advantageously in several regions, or in foreign countries, there are then definite territorial limitations to the market of the individual

36

manufacturer. The extent of these limitations depends on the degree of efficiency the manufacturer can attain relative to competitors producing in other regions.

6. *Character of the market.* -The character of the market is also an important factor in deciding upon the extent of the market and what to do to reach it. In a country like the United States there are three types of markets from the standpoint of location, each with its special needs and wants. These types are the urban, suburban, and rural markets. An urban market because of social pressure, may be a good field for the sale of dinner cloths and evening dresses. A rural market because of special need will offer outlets for heavy and strong shoes and work cloths. The suburban market will evidence a demand for lawn, flower seed, automobiles and porch furniture. For the convenience article like cigarettes the market area will include all three location types. If there is need for special effort in any one of these markets, that fact should certainly be discovered and carefully considered. However, the boundary lines between metropolitan or urban, suburban and rural markets are becoming less hard and fast. The motor truck, the automobile and good roads have done much to break down distinctions formerly existing.

7. *The potentialities of the market.* -In attempting to measure the possibilities of a market for a product it is essential to know the total annual volume of consumption of the product, the per capita consumption, and the particular company's actual share of the total business. The ratio of actual users to logical or potential users can then be determined and means adopted to convert as many possible the logical users into actual users. The replacement factor enters into this calculation. Some products because of their obsolescence are discarded before their usefulness is actually at an end. New ones are purchased because of a change in color or style, or the introduction of an improvement, which makes the old product completely out of vogue. Radios, automobiles, and furniture are typical products in which an estimate of the replacement market is necessary to discover the true market potentialities. On the other hand, a product like and electric range may have practically no possibility of a repeat or replacement sale. In the latter case, the market potentialities lie almost entirely in turning logical users into actual users. The problem is one of inducing the consumer to recognize the need for the article and to stimulate a desire to purchase it. The tendency of the market for a product to increase or decrease must be considered from the standpoint of its bearing upon market potentialities. When a product that fills a fundamental need, like the automobile, comes on the market, there is a reasonable assurance that the tendency will be toward an increasing use. But what is going to be the effect on other products? Wagon and carriage industries were not aware until forty years ago that the tendency in their markets was a decreasing one. Silk and furs for women's attire came very rapidly to the fore because of improved methods of manufacturer and the increased general prosperity of the population. As a result, the cotton and woolen industries had to face a strong competition from these sources. Market research and analysis must give continuous attention to such possibilities.

8. *Market limitations.* -Market potentialities must also be considered in the light of particular factors which exert a limiting influence upon the market for a given product. Some of these factors are:

(a) Purchasing power

(b) Price

(c) Fashion

(d) Cost of product operation

(e) Seasonal and climatic conditions

(f) The second-hand market

9. *Purchasing power and price.* -Purchasing power is an important limiting factor in the per capita consumption of a particular product. Studies of income ranges and typical family budgets will be helpful in any analysis of present and potential per capita consumption. If the price of the product is high these factors assume general market significance because the relationship of the high price to the amount which is available in the typical budget in a specific income range will certainly limit the market. The economist states that the price of a product must be fixed at a point which appeals to the marginal buyer. The price may be so high that only a few can buy. Every lowering of the price will reach new buying strata and create added market opportunities. On the other hand, if the product was intended for the "classes" and not the "masses" a high price is an effective way of limiting market potentialities.'

10. *Fashion.* -The influence of fashion is another factor which may seriously limit market potentialities. At one-time quality was the prime factor considered in making a purchase. To-day, quality is taken for granted, but style is not. Unless a product possesses the style that has been accepted as fashion, its market will be limited to the few who do not care about the vogue. Moreover, the tempo of fashion change is far more rapid to-day than in the past. In most cases a refusal to keep in step with fashion changes will mean a serious market limitation, even though the product concerned possesses valuable quality and performance characteristics and is sold at a very low price.

The forth factor, cost of product operation, is a limiting market factor that is not always given the consideration that it deserves. When automobiles first came in the market the cost of operation was exceedingly high. Chauffeurs were almost a necessity. The cost of repairs and of gasoline and lubricating oil was considerable. Sales were limited largely to the wealthy until the Ford Motor Company set up its mass-production program. The advent of the low-cost, highly standardized car making possible owner driving and cheap repairs coupled with the decreased cost of gasoline and oil, has developed the use of the automobile in America to an extent that has astounded the rest of the world. All along, American automobile manufacturers were able to widen their markets because the cost of running cars were gradually decreased and middle-class families and lower-income families and lower-income groups came rapidly into the purchasing market.

11. *Climatic and measured factors.* -Climatic and seasonal influences are also obvious factors limiting market potentialities. Climate, in particular, determines the extent of almost

every market. Woolen caps are not a fast-moving commodity in Brazil. Heavy rubber galoshes are not greatly in demand in Florida. Coal stoves for heating purposes are not necessities in Southern California. Seasonal factors are likewise essentially limiting factors. Moreover, they complicate the whole task of manufacturing and marketing. Compare, for example, the opportunities and the marketing problems facing the manufacturers, respectively, of lead pencils and men's straw hats. There is no seasonal demand for lead pencils, except perhaps, a slight increase at the opening of the school year. Goods can be moved in a relatively steady stream from the factory through the channels of trade to the points of final consumption.

The manufacturer of men's straw hats, however, has but one season and a very short one. He must estimate seasonal demand twelve months or more in advance and then attempt to schedule production throughout the year. He must arrange to have his wholesale and retail customers (his immediate market) accept a considerable part of his goods long before the consumer wants them, so that he can get money with which to carry on his operations and so that the goods will surely be on hand in his ultimate market when the season opens. He must hazard guesses on the popularity of new styles and risk large losses on them because he has little or no opportunity to try out these styles even in a tentative way. Moreover, he can sell the stock which he has manufactured to meet maximum requirements only if the season brings the normal amount of hot weather.

12. *The second-hand market.* -In a number of cases, the second-hand market operates to limit the market for first-quality goods. For several years, the used-car automobile market has been as important limiting factor in the sale of new cars. It is a factor which is likely to increase in seriousness. Whether it will offset the potentialities of promotion and of changes in design that increase the rate of obsolescence is an important question. The second-hand market limitation has a direct bearing on price and profits. Generally, the used product will have to be taken in exchange in every placement purchase and a price allowance made for the old product. The situation is not without its favorable aspects, however. A wide second-hand market may serve as an educating medium. Users may come into the replacement market for new products solely because of experience with used products of a similar types.

13. *Status of competition.* -Obviously, no survey of market possibilities will be complete without an inquiry into the factor of competition. To ignore competition is to distort the facts regarding the true quantitative market potentialities of a product. A number of questions are important. How many competitors are in the market? How many are in each section of the market? What indirect competition comes from products of a different but related kind? Coffee substitutes compete with coffee. Hot water heaters compete with steam heaters, mechanical refrigerators with ice refrigerators, vacuum cleaners with carpet sweepers. What is the relative marketing strength of each competitor? How much business is each competitor getting? Suppose, for example, a manufacturer discovers that fourteen competitors have preceded him in a territory that naturally should be his. One gets 75 per cent of the business, one gets 10 per cent, and the other twelve divide the remaining minute portion. If the new manufacturer needs 10 per

cent of the business in order to keep his plant running, he may decide that it will be cheaper and easier to go after the business of the trailers rather than to try to make a dent in the trade of the overshadowing leader. It is normally less difficult to enter a market in which there are a few dominant figures and many less important ones than one in which a large number are striving evenly for business. If the leading manufacturer gets only 15 per cent of the total business and if he is closely followed by many others, the new manufacturer who plans for a large output must rank from the outset well up among the leaders if he is to keep his plant busy. This is not an easy task to undertake and the manufacturer attempting it must be well backed by capital and selling strategy. Whatever may be the situation, the market research department should set up some quantitative percentage evaluation of the company's position in the market as compared with competing companies. It should discover and analyze also the reasons back of the effective competition on the part of other manufacturers. These reasons should be pinned down to the definite factors of price, quality, performance, service, transportation, recognition, executive management, patents, and other important items.

14. *Choosing a market objective*. -Every manufacturer, of course, does not attempt to cultivate his entire market. Although in some cases the neglect of a portion of the market is the result of ignorance of its true extent, more often the restriction of activities to only a few of the possible outlets is the result of a conscious marketing policy. Relatively few manufacturers are actually in a position to attempt national marketing. Many who are carrying on extensive programs are spreading themselves too thinly over the whole territory. They could probably reduce their marketing costs and secure greater returns by concentrating their efforts in more restricted areas. In the case of a new product, prudence usually dictates a modest start in a single community, and the gradual extension of coverage as rapidly as marketing campaigns can be brought to bear effectively on wider areas.

The quantitative factors which have been mentioned are important in defining the possible markets, but an examination of the qualitative factors is necessary to decide upon the particular markets which can be served most profitably. Moreover, these qualitative factors will be the most important indicators of the specific sales methods that should be employed. One of the most interesting phases of market analysis is concerned with the attempt to discover the qualitative factors which affect the purchase of a given product by an individual consumer. Marketing is very largely a matter of people and not of stereotyped sales talks, conventional advertising copy and widespread circulation coverage. It is a matter not only of ability to buy but also readiness and willingness to buy.

15. *Principal qualitative market factors*. -The principal qualitative buying factors which affect the purchases of an individual consumer are:

(a) Age

(b) sex

(c) Race

(d) Religion

(e) Occupation

(f) Social standing or class

(g) Knowledge of operating methods

(h) amusements and hobbies

(i) Prejudices

(j) Buying habits

(k) Buying motives

An individual, in making purchases, is inevitably influenced by these factors which represent the effects of heredity, environment, and education. Moreover, taken collectively, individual consumers react alike to any given stimulus.

16. *Age*. -The influence of age as a qualitative factor in marketing is apparent. Products that are necessary and desirable for a child in most cases are not necessary or desirable for grown-ups. Maturity and old age have their special purchasing demands. Moreover, the consumers' freedom of choice varies somewhat with the different age periods. Children up to ten or twelve years of age generally have their decisions made for them by older people. After that they may decide largely for themselves and may begin to influence the decisions of the older members of the family. As old age creeps on, most people who are in a family circle are influenced even in their own purchases by the decisions and choices of the mature but younger members of the family. However, generalizations are hazardous and each product situation must be examined for itself.

17. *Sex*. -In the case of sex as a qualitative marketing factor there is a first, of course, the difference in the fundamental requirements of men and women. Then there is the relative influence that each have on purchases. It has been estimated that the women in the United States make between 80 and 90 per cent of all the ultimate-consumer purchases. One investigator claims to have discovered that the only thing men purchase without the aid of women is collars. There is probably considerable exaggeration in this statement. In any household it will be found usually that the men are consulted on most purchases involving an outlay of money greater that the day-to-day requirements and that men exercise more purchasing influence than is usually recognized. Nevertheless, the point needs careful investigation.

18. *Racial factors*. – Although the United States has been called the melting-pot of nationalities, the fusing fire burns slowly. There are still almost 1,000 foreign language publications printed regularly in the United States. It is estimated that the population of New York is about 70 per cent foreign born or of foreign parentage. Other cities are also compositely populated although the quantitative figures vary. Moreover, many cities are peopled quite largely by some particular race. Any approach to a specific market must take into account this racial factor. The racial peculiarities of our foreign-born population persist often for several

generations. These peculiarities are particularly important in influencing the marketing of foodstuffs. Some have stamped themselves upon our national life. For example, noodles, spaghetti, macaroni, sauerkraut, and goulash are foreign dishes that have become standard additions to the nation's diet.

19. *Religion.* -Religion is diminishing in importance as a qualitative purchasing factor. Unleavened bread, prepared fish, rosaries, homiletic commentaries, Sunday-School supplies, candles, church insignia, communion sets, and similar products find primary markets among people of specific religious faiths. However, they form only a fraction of the total volume of purchases, and the gradual disappearance of strict religious distinctions is lessening the influence of religious differences in marketing.

20. *Occupation.* -The occupation of the consumer is of considerable importance in any analysis of buying factors. A shoe that is to be sold through general stores and that is made for daily wear by the farmer will differ from the shoe made for the clerk in a city office and sold to him through a chain store. In one occupation, overalls may be in demand, in another, smocks, and in still another, leather aprons. Moreover, the painter may demand overalls of cotton cloth in the gray, the locomotive hickory stripes and the subway laborer brown duck. Special products and special materials and colors are in demand for particular industrial occupations. A little investigation will soon discover these occupational preferences.

21. *Class or social position.* –For the manufacturer and distributor of books, picture and works of art, the factor of social standing or class may be important. In any consideration of this factor it should be remembered that culture has very much more to do with a determination of the class to which purchasers belong than does wealth. Frequently, errors are made in giving to much importance to this particular qualitative factor. Many manufacturers and distributors are sacrificing profitable sales opportunities by complacently accepting narrow class markets instead of making actual studies of the problems of possible consumption in wider fields.

22. *Knowledge of operating methods.* -The knowledge of operating methods which ultimate consumers need in order to use a given product effectively may also be a matter for consideration and evaluation. If an electric ironing machine or some similar device is being marketed to housewives, this operating factor must be investigated and means must be arrived at for reducing any limiting influence it may have in marketing of the product.

23. *Hobbies and recreations.* -Hobbies, recreations, and leisure interests may also affect the problem of marketing. Whenever it is discovered that these factors affect the decision to purchase, plans should be formulated to capitalize on the situation. Sales talks and advertising copy which can be directed along such lines sell from the consumer's pint of view.

Because of the growing influence of the golf the two-trouser suit for men, one long, one knicker, has now extended to conservative models beyond the mere sport style. Under the influence of widespread recreational activities, many kinds of sports cloths, such as outing shirts, shorts, slacks, sport jackets, and combinations of these units, have been put on the market in answer to demands.

24. *Market prejudices.* -Market prejudices should also be given consideration. Many of these prejudices are a results of custom and grow out of inherited traditions, and some are the result of unsatisfactory experiences of one type or another. Because of a persistent market prejudice, oleomargarines have only recently come into general use. In the early days, these products were regarded as greasy cooking compounds and did not receive widespread consumer acceptance for table use. In the days when fruits and vegetables were put up in large quantities in the home there was a prejudice against a manufacturers' canned goods because of mistaken ideas on quality, cleanliness and dangers of metallic poisoning. Machine-made garments made slow progress at first against hand-sewed clothing because of the belief, unfounded in fact, that machine work was inferior because it cost less to perform.

25. *Buying habits.* -Habit-man's constant and almost universal urge to repeat the same act-is one of the most vital of the qualitative market considerations. Purchases may be impulsive, reasoned or habitual, but in the majority of cases they are the latter. Deeply-rooted buying habits are difficult to modify or change. What is customary and usual must be discovered in any market survey. As Percival White has pointed out:

For years, New England considered white rubber goods superior in quality to red, while the rest of the country considered red rubber superior to white. Instances of sectional buying habits are many. Green asparagus in Boston, white in Chicago; rubber-stemmed pipes in New England, celluloid in the South, dark cheese in the south, light cheese in the North; cream of tartar in Maine, baking powder in the rest of the country. These are only a few cases.

But buying habits do not concern only the type of product that is customarily purchased. They involve also the amount or unit of product bought, when the purchase will be made. They form the basis of an attitude of acceptance, and insistence. When fully developed and established in relation to a particular product they result in consumer insistence which in its negative aspect means consumer hostility toward directly and indirectly competing products. It is frequently said that if an article contributes to the personal appearance, comfort or health of the person for whom it is purchased, his attachment for it is much stronger than for some other possession of more utility. It is difficult to switch a man from a make and shape of collar that satisfies him. It is much easier to win him over to a new brand of writing ink. Unquestionably, every detail of buying habits that affect the product line or its uses is important to market research.

26. *Buying motives.* -A step beyond buying habits is the factor of buying motives, the "whys" of human behavior. When it is desired to induce people to break away from habitual purchases in order to buy impulsively or through reasoning, the use of appeals to buying m motives is fundamental. Unfortunately, very little thoroughly scientific work has been done on the subject of buying motives so that it is hardly possible to set up a standardized list of motives. The existence of several different schools of thought on the subject of psychology, each school at odds with the others, is retarding progress in discovering and standardizing fundamental buying motives. On the other hand, these various groups are stimulating progress by specializing and experimenting in different phases of the problem of influencing human behavior. One set of consumers' buying motives has been set up by Copeland after a study of a large number of

advertisements. He lists these motives in two groups as follow in his book on "Principles of merchandising":

Emotional

1. Distinctiveness

2. Emulation

3. Economical emulation

4. Pride of personal appearance

5. Pride in appearance of property

6. Social achievement

7. Proficiency

8. Expression in artistic taste

9. Happy selection of gifts

10. Ambition

11. Romantic interest

12. Maintaining and preserving health

13. Cleanliness

14. Proper care of children.

15. Satisfaction of the appetite

16. Pleasing the sense of taste.

17. Securing personal comfort

18. Alleviation of laborious tasks

19. Security from danger

20. Pleasure or recreation

21. Entertainment

22. Obtaining opportunity for greater leisure

23. Securing home comfort

Rational

24. Handiness

25. Efficiency in operation or use

26. Dependability in use

27. Dependability in quality

28. Reliability in auxiliary service

29. Durability

30. Enhancement of earnings

31. Enhancing productivity of property

32. Economy in use

33. Economy of purchase

The list is extensive but not all-inclusive. It is suggestive, and should be used in that sense. Carefully-conducted surveys applied to particular products should determine the important buying motives for purchases under established conditions and should be used to discover the proper shade of phrasing to express an appeal that has proved to be effective.

MARKET RESEARCH-EFFICIENSY AND COST INVESTIGATIONS

1. *Efficiency and cost investigations*. -One phase of market research that is often completely neglected is the execution of specialized efficiency and cost investigations. Even in cases where the need for such studies may be recognized their value is greatly underemphasized. These investigations are concerned primarily with the analysis and evaluation of particular marketing methods and with application to those methods of the searching technique of scientific inquiry. Efficiency and cost investigations range from such a topic as: A General Time Study of Salesmen's Operations, to What Constitutes a Profitable Wholesale Order, or An Investigation of Color in a Direct Mail Advertising Campaign. Unfortunately, this type of particularized inquiry is seldom performed, because the broader and more general surveys which determine the basic facts for a new marketing campaign, all too frequently occupy the whole time and energy of the market research department.

2. *Importance of efficiency investigations*. -Unquestionably, one of the most important tasks of marketing management is the effective control and reduction of marketing costs. High costs are due just as often to wasteful routine methods as to vaguely defined campaign objectives, "hunch" planning, and illogical general marketing policies. Careful analysis will point out the needless operations, lost motions, and other forms of waste. Research will indicate the methods that will lower cost of specific marketing programs.

Since the variety of problems that may arise is so great, it is not possible to present any detailed statement of what to do or how to do it. About all that can be accomplished in this discussion is to point out what the technique of scientific inquiry involves in general and to indicate some of the more important marketing topics that call for detailed study. Consequently, the purpose of this chapter is to suggest possibilities rather than too present guaranteed working formulas. The point of view is that discovering and preventing marketing wastes at their source, rather than that of salvaging or utilizing waste which has already occurred. Applying waste-prevention plans to routine marketing methods cannot be described truthfully as one of the most interesting of management's many problems. "Plugging the leaks" lacks the thrill of competition, and the enthusiasm that results from discovering how to make more sales. But making sales may mean little, so far as profits are concerned, if the resulting gains are dissipated by careless and wasteful methods.

3. *The scientific technique of inquiry.* – The scientific approach to the study of effectiveness and cost of the particular marketing method involves analysis, classification, synthesis or combining and building up, and measurement. For example, take one particular problem such as might be indicated by the question: What is the task of personal salesmanship in this particular business enterprise? Certainly, the investigation of this question must start with an analysis of the unit operations now being performed by the salesmen in the field. This analysis almost immediately intertwines with classification, because important unit operations must be separated from unimportant operations. Furthermore, analysis and classification must go beyond what is now being done, to list and classify operations that should be performed, but that, for some reason, are not being performed. In the same way, close analyses must be made of the operations now being performed, to eliminate the nonessentials. Then, before synthesis can be used to build up essential standards the time and effort devoted to various unit operations must be measured. Standards may then be built up but further measurement is necessary to discover the best way to execute the individual unit operations. Even after suggested standards have been established, measurement must still be applied to determine the accuracy of the standards and to judge the effectiveness of the medium adopted.

4. *Standards of work.* -The aim and purpose of research into matters of efficiency and cost is to establish standard methods of work. Since a standard represents the best method of performing a certain operation under existing conditions, it implies effectiveness and economy. Standards, or goals of achievement, should take into account both theory and practice. They should be built up on the basis of analysis, classification and measurement. In the field of manufacturing, the principal devices for measuring operations are time studies and motion studies. Although these two types of tools cannot be used in the same manner to measure unit marketing operations, yet they can and should be used to some extent. Due allowance must be made for the fact that the standards established for marketing methods cannot be so rigid as standards for manufacturing operations. More leeway must be provided for variation. Nevertheless, marketing standards must be stable enough to make constant revision unnecessary.

5. *The necessity for system.* -when standards have been perfected by the scientific methods of analysis, classification, measurement and synthesis or building up, the next task is to provide a systematic procedure of work. Details of routine should be laid down is standard-practice instructions. These instructions are merely written statements of the way in which jobs are done. They should include outlines which indicate where the particular job begins, where it leaves off, and how it ties in with related tasks. They should cover comprehensively he main steps pf the operation, even though they may not be able to set up in minute detail just how each step is to be performed or to suggest exact sequences. Moreover, they should indicate schedules in the sense of providing desirable but flexible time limits. Finally, system necessitates some provision for work-progress observations and reports. These reports will not be needed in all cases, of course, and just where they are essential can be determined only through the study of the particular circumstances involved. Nevertheless, periodic work-progress measurements give

the true picture of what is going on and are frequently essential to the control of a particular marketing method. Moreover, they show up the need for any change in established standards.

6. *Qualitative factors are important.* - The steps that are necessary in efficiency and cost investigations have ben stated very generally. The importance of any one or of any group will vary widely over a number of specialized investigations. For example, some investigations, at least, will deal necessarily in the main with qualitative factors which cannot be measured accurately. In such cases, observation, analysis, and classification will be the important steps.

7. *Sources of special problems.* -The next question of importance deals with the type of problem or subject-matter for these specialized investigations. The number of such problems is legion, but where shall they be sought out? Most of the problems that lend themselves to specialized efficiency and cost investigations grow out of the methods used by the manufacturer in marketing his product line to his immediate market, and his relationship to the problem faced by his middlemen distributors in handing the goods on to his ultimate market. For example, if a manufacturer is selling directly to wholesalers or jobbers his important problems of cost are concerned with:

(a) The sales-making methods of his field sales force

(b) His trade advertising methods

(c) His consumer advertising methods

(d) His missionary or service methods of assisting the wholesaler to market his line

(e) His missionary or service methods of helping the retailer.

Of the above, the third factor alone is exclusively an ultimate-market factor. Moreover, if the manufacturer is not engaged in marketing a branded product, this factor may not be present at all. Likewise, in the same situation, the fifth factor, assisting the retailer, may also be completely absent.

8. *How the field salesman spends his time.* -In connection with the work of the field sales force, a number of special problems present themselves. First, there is a question of the way in which the salesman spends his time in the field. A careful survey of this problem is an attempt to analyze just what must be done and how much time each unit operation should take will be of a considerable value. Economical and effective standards may be set up and supervising systems may be suggested which will cut down materially the existing wastes or costs. Any details study of this factor of the salesman's time is likely to reveal astonishing conditions. One such investigation made by the Lowe Brothers Company disclosed that in the case of a single salesman:

(a) His cost per call was $18.70

(b) He called upon one agent once who bought not $1 worth of merchandise from the company during the entire year

(c) A town in which no sales were made had been visited seven times at an expense of $131

(d) One account was called on 52 times at a selling expense greatly in excess of the proceeds made on the account

(e) One agency was called on once, the sales from which amounted to $18.20 and the cost of call amounted to $18.70

(f) Another agency buying $1,850 worth of merchandise was called on once

(g) Another customer buying $208 was not called on at all

In a general time selling the Dennison Manufacturing Company discovered that their salesmen were distributing their time as follows: 40 per cent to traveling, 20 per cent to waiting, 25 per cent to clerical and miscellaneous duties, and only 15 per cent to sales conversation in the actual presence of prospects or customers. Traveling methods and methods of making out sales reports and records were immediately analyzed. New methods and new time standards were established which provided for an increase in the actual selling time to 30 per cent of the total working time. It is only through such studies that economical and effective standards for the number of salesman's calls per day, the number of sales in relation to the number of calls, the frequency of calls upon the better accounts, the frequency of calls upon the poorer accounts, and other factors, can be determined at all scientifically.

9. *Salesmen's compensation.* -When studies have indicated the details that should constitute the salesman's task the methods of compensating sales efforts may also be reviewed. The effectiveness of any bonus, credit-point, or efficiency rating plan that may be employed should be investigated. Standards established for sales efforts as distinguished from non-selling field duties should be analyzed from the standpoint of the compensation actually earned by individual salesmen. In general, where the salesman is expected to perform many different activities, some methods of rewarding his accomplishments other than a mere commission on sales or a flat salary are necessary. Rating indices such as the following can be employed to measure results: Number of calls made, number of large profit sales, number of new accounts opened during definite periods, number of average profit sales, total volume of sales, annual increase in sales volume, number of letters of complaint received from the salesman's territory. After a thorough study of the problem, a compensation plan may be evolved which meets directly the needs of the salesmen and of the house.

10. *Salesmen's expense accounts.* -In a similar way, a salesmen's expense accounts may be studied. Present parties should be analyzed and classified in the light of the practices of other companies. Whether or not the expense accounts ae padded, whether or not the expenses

allowed really cover the activities required and provide the salesmen with an adequate net compensation are important questions. In fact, a periodic survey of this problem is practically imperative to prevent waste due to unnecessary expenditures and dissatisfaction among the salesmen because of too restrictive a policy.

11. *Miscellaneous problems of field sales.* -While these particular problems are among the most important subjects that pertain to the work of the field sales force and that need special efficiency and cost investigations, they by no means exhaust the whole list of personal sales topics. Questions of recruiting, selecting, training, stimulating and controlling salesmen may also be broken down into specific problems for scientific inquiry. Consider, for example, the matter of recruiting. A study of the records of salesmen were obtained may be very enlightening and serve to establish standard sources which can be used effectively and economically in making additions to the field sales personnel. One such study made by a large grocery wholesaler resulted in a policy of recruiting wholesale salesmen from behind the retail grocery counter rather than from men of wholesale selling experience either in the grocery or in other lines.

12. *Problems of advertising to the trade.* -Special surveys may also be useful in establishing standards by means of which the effectiveness of trade advertising can be measured. The amount spent for trade-paper advertising, the total circulation of the magazines used, the number of impressions run of each advertisement, the circulation of each publication used multiplied by the number of times the advertisement appears in it, the cost per inquiry received, cost per sale or per new customer and other factors may be combined and examined in various ways to establish a standard method of measuring advertising efficiency. Again, a study may be made of the methods in use for setting up the appropriation for trade advertising in an attempt to eliminate purely rule-of-thumb decisions. The method of dividing up the appropriation for trade advertising may be investigated to establish standard ratios of expenditures to be made for direct mail advertising as compared to the advertising in trade magazines. The aim of these special surveys should be to discover the best method of accomplishing the particular task. The investigations should not be confines merely to a recording of the results of a present method. It is fundamental, of course, to find out just what method is being used to set up and apportion the appropriation for trade advertising but the more important purpose of a special study is to establish the best method or technique that can be used in carrying out a particular marketing operation effectively and economically.

13. *Allocating advertising costs.* -The same general problems present themselves for study in connection with advertising to the ultimate market. Both in the case of advertising to the immediate market and to the ultimate market, these problems are important entirely aside from the question of whether the particular seller prepares and places his own advertising or uses an advertising agency. If the seller does not use an agency many additional matters must be surveyed in the search for efficient methods. For instance, the whole question of charging advertising expense to the several items in a "family" or line of products may need investigation. Or a particular phase of this problem such as the distribution of advertising overhead to the several items in the product line may require study. The amount of overhead advertising costs

may be assigned to each product on some time base or ratio. Obviously, a given product that, in actual advertising outlay for space in periodicals, for car cards, or for dealer helps, may involve a relatively high total expense, may require comparatively little time for the preparation of copy and layout and for general supervision. Conversely, another product may incur a comparatively low expense for space, but consume a large amount of advertising department work. Standard methods of measuring this time factor should be established.

14. *Miscellaneous advertising problems*. -In addition to these problems of advertising appropriations, charges to individual products, and the like, the seller who prepares and places his own advertising can carry on many additional investigations of particular tasks that have to do with copy, layout, illustrations, color, typography, the selection of mediums, and duplicate of circulation. There is little excuse for any failure to keep the research department busy. Between the more elaborate surveys of products, markets, and competition, these special problems should be made the subjects of efficiency and cost investigations. If, for any reason, the research department cannot devote a great deal of time to this latter type of inquiry, it should compile, classify and present to the advertising personnel all the available individual studies on these subjects that have been made by other research departments, and by colleges and universities, advertising agencies and trade association bureaus. Journals featuring research in experimental and applied psychology should be carefully scanned or the reports of these special investigations. Every bit of data that has to do with advertising techniques should be put into reference form for the consultation and use of advertising department.

15. *Profitable and unprofitable orders*. -When we turn to the manufacturer's immediate market as distinguished from his marketing technique of reaching that market, one very important subject for efficiency and cos study becomes apparent. Whether the manufacturer sells direct to wholesalers, or direct to retailers, or both, the problem arises of determining what constitutes a profitable order. It must not be assumed that small orders are not profitable. Nor must the marketing management subscribe too quickly to the doctrine that while many accounts do not pay their way nothing should be done about it because "great oaks from little acorns grow." Certainly it will pay to find out what constitutes a profitable order, and which of the smaller accounts will be likely to remain unprofitable because that possess very little potential for growth. The "acorns" must be picked over.

16. *What one manufacturer's study revealed*. -One such detailed study on the part of the manufacturer revealed the fact the direct sales expense per dollar of sales to customers buying under $5,000 worth of merchandise annually was $0.3561 as compared with a direct sales expense per dollar of sales of $0.0312 to customers buying over $5,000 worth of merchandise annually. An extension of the same analysis of the large-customer and small customer groups showed and operating profit of $0.0993 per dollar of sales in the case of small customers. Fortunately for this company, $775,000 worth of sales were made to the large-customer group and only $25,000 worth of sales to the small-customer group. Obviously, the sales to large customers carried the burden of selling the small customers, and this is a condition that needs to be watched. Classifications of potentially profitable accounts and of accounts that will never be in a position to use more than a small amount of the product line must be set up. The latter type

of customers may be handled by mail, telephone or some method other than personal calls. Measurement, analysis, classification, and a building up of adequate methods must be applied to this whole problem to develop profitable standards of procedure.

17. *The minimum order.* -The size of the order which is the standard minimum for profitable acceptance will unquestionably have a definite effect on marketing costs. The aim in setting the standard should be to decide upon a minimum order which is small enough to secure extensive distribution and which is at the same time large enough to constitute an economical unit for the manufacturer to handle and large enough to make the middleman distributor feel that it is worth backing with special marketing effort. Even after the minimum order standard is set, periodic surveys may be necessary to watch the results. At times a large minimum can be established during the introduction of a new product. As soon as it is introduced, the minimum standard may have to be reduced. In other cases, during the period of introduction small minimum order standards may be necessary, while later arrangements may increase the size of the minimum order. The experience of one company which has been very successful in keeping down its marketing costs is summarized as follows by Ray Giles, writing in *Advertising and Selling*:

On marketing a new specialty, the minimum order accepted was for three gross units. Calculations showed that the average dealer should dispose of this quantity within three weeks. The salesman called every two weeks. At the start only the better dealers were wanted. The minimum order was made big enough to keep out the chapter and nondesirable class of trade.

The success of this specialty caused competitive products to disappear. The minimum order was cut in half to get the product in stores which otherwise might supply competitors with outlets.

In warmer parts of the country this product is sold in still smaller quantities to safeguard the consumer against getting stale goods.

18. *The middleman and his minimum order.* -This problem of the minimum order is not confined to the manufacturer alone. It is of the utmost importance to the middleman distributor as well, and he, too, is applying special surveys to its solution. One such study that was conducted by a wholesale hardware dealer established the conclusion that in order to be profitable a retail account must be made up of at least $25 order per month, or two $20 orders per month, or three $15 orders per month. This study was followed by a careful analysis of all the accounts on the wholesaler's list and then management took action. One-half of the customers were eliminated, one-third of the wholesaling territory was given up, and the stock carried was reduced one-third. In spite of this drastic action and the fact that the total annual business dropped, the annual profits were greatly increased.

19. *Study of the wholesaler's problems.* -Another question of importance to the manufacturer in relation to his immediate market is a special study of the wholesaler's problem

in marketing the manufacturer's particular line of goods. This type of study is highly qualitative as quantitative in character. Likewise, it involves an analysis of competition. The fundamental questions here are:

(a) How valuable is the manufacturer's product line to the wholesaler?

(b) How can it be made more valuable?

Normally, a product line will be valuable to a wholesaler because of volume, long profit, high price, frequency of sale, exclusive franchise, the help the particular line may give in selling other goods, or novelty. These factors and others should be listed and analyzed as they apply to the particular situation and as they compare with competing lines. If makers of competitive goods seem able to secure greater cooperation from the wholesaler, the reasons for the condition must be traced down to basic problems which can be made the subject of special studies. Some of the problems that a particular line of goods may present to the wholesaler are problems of large investment, unwieldy stock, too extensive a line, slow movement, difficulty in storing, difficulty in delivering, awkwardness in handling, questionable assortments, and spoilage, or deterioration, or both.

20. *Evaluation of service to the wholesaler.* -A careful analysis of these factors leads directly into a study of the effectiveness of the wholesalers' salesmen and of the adequate means to assist them. It is important for the manufacturer to have exact knowledge as whether his product line is sold by all of the wholesalers' salesmen or only certain men, whether the product is sold individually or with related goods, and whether the wholesalers' salesmen can explain and demonstrate the selling points of the product line. On the quantitative side, it is desirable to have information as to the records of the wholesalers' salesmen in selling the product line to few or many retail outlets, in small or large quantities, and in few or many sizes. With such data in hand, the manufacturer can undertake a special study to ascertain the methods that will be most effective and economical as aids to the wholesaler's salesmen. These aids include: Lectures or talks at jobbers' headquarters, periodical sales meeting with the wholesalers' salesmen, moving pictures, house organs, bulletin boards in wholesalers' sales offices, individual or group training by the manufacturer's zone instructors, prize contests, sales manuals, sample cases, and special bonuses paid by the manufacturer. These methods may be tried out in various territories, their results checked and measured, and standard practice procedures established.

21. *Study of the retailer's problems.* -The same specific possibilities of study exist in the manufacturer's retail outlets, whether he is reaching the retail market directly and exclusively, or whether he is reaching it in part through the wholesale middlemen and in part directly. The retailer, too, provides intensive selling cooperation or withholds it because of very definite factors that may be present or absent in the product line. Such matters as an attractive unit of sale, an easily-obtained frequency of sale, the consumer's wide familiarity with the product line, and the helpfulness of the product line in selling other lines, and positive factors making for cooperation. Problems of large investment, bulky stocks, and unusual difficulties in storing, delivering, displaying, demonstrating, and servicing are, on the other hand, negative factors which lessen retailing cooperation. Both types must be analyzed and measured. Means of

providing practical sales assistance and retail sales instruction must be studied in terms of efficiency and cost. Moreover, studies of the effectiveness of marketing through different types of retailers are important. There are many special types of retailers but few types of wholesalers and jobbers. Sales through department stores, for example, may show lower total cost per unit than sales through exclusive specialty stores for the same product. Before costs can be reduced they must be known and special studies present the best opportunity for their determination.

22. *The necessity for special knowledge*. -The subjects that have been suggested are merely a few of those warranting special study to assure effectiveness and economy in marketing. The aim has been merely to present the necessity for this type of inquiry and to outline the field for such investigation. Broadly speaking, there are only two ways to reduce costs and prevent wastes in marketing. One is to devise standard methods that will sell more goods without increasing the marketing expenditures. The other is to spend less money to market the same volume of goods. Knowledge of every phase or marketing is necessary to develop and establish the best and most economical methods, and such knowledge comes only from carefully conducted studies.

Lecture Three

MARKET FORECASTING- FUNDAMENTALS

1. *Cause of business waste*. -One of the chief causes of business waste is the failure to estimate or forecast sales possibilities in order to coordinate these possibilities with production schedules. Production, in the sense of making goods, is not an end of business effort in itself. Goods are manufactured to be sold. Producing or manufacturing goods faster than they can be disposed of to ultimate consumers intensifies competition and usually results in wasteful advertising and "high-pressure" personal salesmanship.

2. *Overemphasis on production*. -For the past fifty years the processes of making goods have been steadily improved and production costs have been decreased. The standardization of the methods of large-scale production and the application of scientific management to industrial operations have reduced manufacturing costs and lowered the resultant prices to the consumer. But in many instances the increase in production brought about by scientific management and mass production has been followed by wasteful and frenzied marketing. In such cases the cost of finding new markets and of intensively cultivating old ones has sometimes counterbalanced completely the savings due to the scientific methods of large-scale production. Efficiencies in manufacturing that are not evaluated in terms of the possibilities of the ultimate-consumer sales, may throw an almost impossible task upon a very efficient marketing department. Mismanaged and uncoordinated production may seriously damage or even render entirely futile marketing plans that are correct in principle, accurate and meticulous in detail, and logical and thorough in operation.

3. *Market forecasting as a remedy*. -The question of what can be done to reduce this sort of what can be done to reduce this sort of waste is all-important. Certainly, American business cannot return to pre-war manufacturing standards. It must maintain the present standards of production efficiency. More than that, it must be prepared to accept the new inventions and the

new manufacturing methods and processes that are being developed almost daily. The most economic solution to this problem is not entirely a high-powered competitive effort to speed up marketing in order to sell all the goods which more efficient factories are able to produce. It is far more a matter of working out a proper coordination between factory output and the carefully determined possibilities of consumer sales. Hence, we have a very definite need for market forecasting.

4. *Present status of market forecasting.* -The difficulties in the way of accurate market forecasting are many. Very little is available in the form of written records that furnish the results of particular forecasting methods. It will take a long time to build up a body of principles and rules because of the wide variety of factors which are present over any extensive range of product lines. Nevertheless, a considerable amount of experimenting is going on and empirically-determined methods are being used with some degree of success. Many of these methods are crude and imperfect measures of sales possibilities. Others appear to answer with reasonable adequacy the purposes for which they are intended. In spite of confusion in the field of market forecasting, the outlook for considerable improvement in methods is good. The necessity for some reasonable method for each product line is growing and is providing the incentive for experimentation.

5. *General principles of forecasting.* -Any examination of the problem of market forecasting should begin with a statement of elementary but basic rules. These rules or principles must be borne in mind in attempting to evolve a method of marketing forecasting for a particular product line. As a matter of fact, these simple rules are about the only rules inclusive enough to apply to apply to the problem of market forecasting over the whole range of possible products for which definite methods are necessary. Moreover, these fundamental principles indicate very clearly the limitations of market forecasting in the sense of possibilities of complete accuracy. These rules will be discussed in the following paragraphs. They are stated, in part, in the phraseology adopted by the American Marketing Association.

6. *Accuracy of prediction and pertinent facts.* -In the first place, it should be plain that an accurate prediction is dependent on knowledge of pertinent facts, and that accuracy of the prediction will ordinarily bear a direct relation to the supply of information. This principal emphasizes the necessity for the collection, classification and tabulation of data.

Much of the information that may be desired to serve as a basis for forecasting may be very difficult to obtain. Nevertheless, it must be obtained in quantity and consistently. The job of collecting it may be a part of the work of the research department and when it is, there should be a closest and most friendly cooperation between the forecasting personnel and the research personnel. On the other hand, much of this work may be compiling and tabulating data from regularly-published statistical source materials. In such cases, the problem of collection is minimized. However, the ease of securing certain types of statistical information should not be allowed to preclude the collection of additional data which may be pertinent.

7. *Specific factors that cannot be predicted.* -In the second place, it should be clear that the purely uncontrollable and unforeseeable factors in a future situation cannot be predicted in their application to a specific case. Some margins of safety will be necessary in setting up particular estimates. Any number of special and local conditions such as floods in the Mississippi Valley, unusually cold weather, drought or excessive rains over a large geographical area, abnormal booms like the Florida real estate bubble, may have a definite effect on individual territories. Such conditions can hardly be anticipated or predicted by statistical formula. When such factors are already present in a territory, their effect can, of course, be estimated and arbitrary territorial adjustments can be made for them in using the general method of prediction.

8. *The effect of the number of conditioning factors.* -If sales are influenced by comparatively few factors, the problem of prediction may be relatively simple. The more conditional factors and the more indices there are that relate directly to market possibilities, the less accurate will be the prediction. It is exceedingly difficult to predict the results of the operation of many varied forces. If many of the variables which are used as indices are highly complicated, the task of forecasting may become so intricate as to present a considerable number of opportunities for error.

9. *The assumption of recurrence.* -All forecasting is based upon the additional principle that a phenomenon which has occurred in the past under certain conditions will occur in the future under similar conditions. A great deal of care must be exercised to make sure that conditions actually are the same whenever the happenings of the past are used as a basis for comparison and identical prediction.

Conditions seldom remain the same for any length of time. Changes, obvious or subtle, usually take place. Consequently, the forecasting personnel must practice constant vigilance in noting changes in old factors and the appearance of new and modifying factors.

10. *The influence of time.* -Another simple and plain forecasting principle is that the nearer the event is to the time of prediction, the more accurate the prediction is likely to be. Short-term forecasts are far more accurate than long-term estimates because the former do not permit of some many unforeseeable happenings and because on the short-time basis the comparative influences of various factors can be estimated more readily.

Thus, the General Motors Corporation, for instance, prepares a forecast once a month for each of the four succeeding months, and then every day during the current month it calculates its position. It is not possible to forecast accurately very far ahead since sales possibilities depend so largely on concurrent developments within the entire business situation during the intervening period.

In most situations, the long-term forecast will show many errors in its detailed predictions even though it may be reasonably accurate in pointing out general trends.

11. *The course of variations.* -Still another principle of forecasting is that the more rhythmic the course of events, the more accurate the prediction. In most businesses the sales vary considerably from month to month or from season to season. It is clear that when these

variations adhere to some regular or rhythmic course, the problem of prediction is much simpler than when the sales fluctuate widely up and down without rhyme or reason. In the case of automobiles, for example, the spring months always have been the months of heaviest retail purchases. Although automobiles are in service all the year around there has been a pronounced trend towards the closed car, these factors have not materially altered the seasonal rhythm of sales.

12. *The forecasting personnel.* -Finally, the accuracy of market forecasting will depend in very large measure upon the skill, knowledge, and detached point of view of the forecasting personnel. If there is any tendency to err either on the optimistic or the pessimistic side the forecasts will inevitably be inexact. If the forecasting personnel does not possess knowledge and skill, the whole procedure will amount to little more than guesswork. Certainly, there are enough limitations on the accuracy of market forecasting without imposing the task upon personnel which is unfitted to attack the problem. The job of forecasting involves the interpretation of data as well as its collection. Only an intelligent and skillful personnel thoroughly conversant with marketing problems and statistical techniques can correlate the various factors and extract logical inferences from confused masses of data.

13. *Basic market units.* -One of the first and most vital points to be determined in an effort to devise a reasonably accurate system of market forecasting is a definite market unit. Some geographical unit of the total market should be settled upon and recognized as the basic territory upon which forecasts will be built. Sales accomplishments and trends can then be measured within the individual unit. The whole purpose is to establish certain units of area concerning which sales possibilities may be forecast and with which sales possibilities may be forecast and with which actual sales and sales efforts in terms of expense may be compared.

14. *The evolution of the "trading area."* -Political divisions of market territory have, in general, proved to be unsatisfactory market units. The state is too large. It almost always includes several different "markets," each one of which deserves individual study. There is a definite need to break the territory down into smaller units. Consequently, many business enterprises are estimating their markets by countries or "trading areas." The tendency in the direction of the use of a trading-area unit is quite pronounced because of the manufacturer's unit sales districts have no more respect for county lines than they have for state boundaries. In this age of good roads, widespread automobile ownership, and low cost bus transportation, buyers travel across county and state lines to do their purchasing as they never did in the past. The county, in and of itself, is too small a market unit. The realization of this fact has resulted in a widespread effort to establish trading areas that will not be based primarily upon the political boundary lines.

15. *The county and the trading area.* -However, one fundamental difficulty with the selection of a market unit without regard for political boundary lines is that such a decision may restrict the amount of reliable data which can be collected with respect to that particular unit. Most of the available data that may be desirable in market forecasting, such as population statistics, income tax returns, and the like, is collected and compiled according to political divisions. Fairly complete and reliable statistics, for example, are available with respect to

county units. Accordingly, in the set-up of most trading areas, the county unit is utilized as much as possible. In the majority of cases whole counties are included in the various areas but are grouped according to the influence of some particular trading center. This adherence to the county unit appears advisable in many business enterprises, because of the forecasting importance attached to current influencing market factors such as population, buying power, sales outlets, advertising coverages, and similar items. Certainly, where it is held necessary to measure these factors statistically and with some frequency, county statistics are essential because they are frequently revised by agencies outside of the individual business enterprise. Trading areas, of course, have been set up which are not confined to groups of counties but which cut through county lines. Many of these suggested trading areas are carefully worked out and are based upon an accurate compilation of statistical data with respect to purchasing power, population, and the like. Their principal disadvantage, however, is that the complied data will soon get out of date and that, in many cases, such surveys offer no guarantee of regular revision and reissue.

16. *Different types of studies available*. -All of the trading area studies which are available, and their number is growing, have their merits and undoubtedly represent helpful and constructive work in supplying market data. Nevertheless, each study has been made up in a different way and for different purposes. Each study splits the national market into a particular number of areas. Some studies are based on newspaper circulation, some on territories covered by jobbers, and some upon transportation facilities, freight and trucking rates, and geographical characteristics. In some cases, state lines have been cut as well as county lines. In other instances, the trading areas fall entirely within the boundaries of the individual states and are composed of a group of counties grouped arbitrarily about a major trading community.

17. Ready-made areas seldom suitable. – No one single set of trading areas can be applied to any considerable range of the product lines and serve for each and all as an effective listing of market units which are basic to reasonably accurate market forecasting. The trading areas for convenience products will differ considerably from those for specialty goods. The trading areas that are useful to the manufacturer who sells directly to the retailer throughout the nation will differ from the trading areas of the manufacturer who sells directly to the jobber and who desires general jobbing distribution. In most cases, a practical system of trading areas must be worked out for the particular company and for the particular line concerned. Any delineation of trading areas will not be identical for any extensive range of consumers' goods. The areas for the various products will overlap and usually will not even be concentric about the "mother" trading city. The individual manufacturer who wishes to devise an accurate system of market forecasting cannot escape logically the necessity of determining his own particular market unit or trading area. The only practical value of a trading area is for the individual business enterprise, seeking to discover potential sales possibilities and to measure its operations against potentials.

18. *Influence of system of distribution*. -Enough has been said to indicate that the establishment of trading areas is not merely a question of adopting and using ready-made market units, but a highly complex matter of working out areas that fit the seller's own particular problem. Just how this can be accomplished can be stated only in generalities. Obviously, if a

manufacturer is selling directly to retailers and through this distributive channel alone, his particular trading areas are fairly easy to determine. A concern like Swift and Company, which sells directly to the retail trade through about 400 carefully-located branch houses, each one of which has its definite territory, will have a fairly easy problem in setting up marketing areas. The same is true of a manufacturer who markets his goods through exclusive jobbers.

The very fact that individual jobbers are given exclusive selling franchises in their own jobbing territories makes it possible to define marketing areas by area to the respective jobbers. On the other hand, a manufacturer who has general jobbing distribution and sells through two or more kinds of jobbers faces a much more complicated undertaking. He may, for instance, market his goods through drug jobbers, grocery jobbers, and jobbers or wholesalers who specialize in selling to general stores in country towns. Since most surveys appear to show that drug jobbing territories are approximately twice as large as grocery jobbing territories, the problem of defining clearly the proper market unit is anything but easy. If, in addition, the manufacturer also sells directly to chain stores, retail buying syndicates, or department stores, in the same territory in which he sells directly to chain stores, retail buying syndicates, or department stores, in the same territory in which he sells to jobbers, the question of establishing trading areas becomes even more intricate. Chain stores, for example, will have their own wholesale warehouses from which they distribute to individual stores, and the territories covered from these warehouse centers will not be likely to correspond at all to the usual jobbing areas.

This particular method of distribution used by the individual manufacturer is one of the most important determining or conditioning factors in establishing a logical and usable market unit.

19. *Analysis of present situation necessary.* -The manufacturer must be give considerable thought to his method of distribution as it affects the problem of defining market areas. He should consider the location of the branch warehouses which he has already established and from which he delivers stock to wholesalers, or to retailers, or to both. He should analyze carefully his present sales districts and the field territories which are now being covered by his salesmen. Also, he should give due weight to the location to the branch offices of competing manufacturers and their defined territories. By cost studies of the general type suggested in and earlier chapter, he should evaluate his profitable market units of sale and delivery. Moreover, he should give special thought to his market as a whole, to ascertain the size of trading areas that may be practical. If his distribution is uneven as far as the whole market is concerned, it may be advisable to set up small territories in one part of the country and larger territories in other sections.

20. *Other factors affecting trading areas.* -Other problem factors of defining service areas are:

(a) The nature of the product

(b) Transportation and physical factors

(c) Individual salesman and company coverage

(d) The time required for the average sale

(e) The need for service

(f) The nature of the distributors.

In the case of products that are bulky the territory surrounding a "mother" trading center probably will be less extensive than in the case of products of smaller bulk. Transportation may influence the size of the marketing area because of the nature of the product and the railroad and highway facilities available. Trading areas usually will be smaller in sections of a state where good roads are few in number r where rail facilities are poor. Likewise, the degree in which a particular company has been able to establish itself in a particular territory may affect the size of the trading area. Consideration must be given to the task before the individual salesman in the proposed delineation of an area. Closely connected with this factor is the matter of time required for an average sale. Some product lines can be sold on a one-call basis but others may require a number of successive solicitations. Physical conditions, therefore, are not the only factors which limit what the individual salesman can do. The need for rapid and efficient service to the territory is another obvious determining factor affecting the size of the trading area.

Finally, the nature of the wholesale and retail distributors will have its influence. A distributor who is progressive and who believes in providing special service and in promoting sales will supply a larger area than a distributor who merely accepts what patronage falls to his lot.

21. *Tools essential to market forecasting.* -The tools essential to market forecasting are:

(A) Accurate and comprehensive records of past and current market performance

(b) Sound but necessarily arbitrary methods for the evaluation of competition

(c) Proved market indices.

The detailed data necessary to provide these forecasting tools will be obtainable in part from the records of the company's operations and in part from external sources. The principal external sources are governmental publications, privately-operated statistical services, financial journals, trade journals, trade associations, mercantile agencies, publishing houses, advertising agencies, newspaper and magazine research departments, addressing companies and directory publishers.

22. *Internal marketing records.* -The company's internal performance records are of considerable service in the work of market forecasting. Entirely apart from the possibilities of using internal records of accomplishment to measure sales, selling expense and advertising against forecasts to locate the weak spots in market distribution, these records of past and current

performance are essential to the verification and correct weighing of individual market indices used in making forecasts. It is seldom possible to get away completely from the experience of past performance. Many types of marketing statistics should be complied by the market research department for possible use in forecasting. In general, the marketing records should show:

(a) Sales by salesmen

(b) Sales by products including sizes, types, and styles

(c) Sales by agencies and branches

(d) sales by territories, trading areas, towns, cities, and counties.

These records are fundamental to comparisons with potential accomplishments. Of course, they should be set up in a form suitable for comparing, weighing, and evaluating the specific groups according to details of the forecast. This necessity means usually that they must be reduced to a percentage basis. Many other internal records may also be kept and some of them will have more than an occasional use. Such additional records may include:

(a) Sales by packages, pounds, yards, gallons, etc., as well as by dollars

(b) Bulk sales

(c) Sales under secondary brand names

(d) Sales under jobbers' or private brand names

(e) Sales by price ranges

(f) Sales by jobbers

(g) Sales directly made to retailers and their possible divisions

(h) Sales made to profitable customers on a monthly, quarterly, or seasonal basis

(i) Other record clarifications of a miscellaneous type.

Since such records cost money to set up and to keep up to date, they should be considered carefully from the viewpoint of necessity and from the standpoint of designing the respective forms and records so that as much as possible of the clerical labor of analysis may be saved.

23. *Use of internal records in forecasting.* -Perhaps the crudest method of setting up a future sales goal is to increase arbitrarily the performance of the past year. To vary this procedure by using the average performance of several years and then adding a certain

percentage of increases equally crude. Such methods do not forecast actual market possibilities. They set up merely arbitrary goals. Moreover, they assume the continuance of the *status quo*. The whole process of increasing from year to year the sales estimates by arbitrary percentages preserves and carries along the weaknesses of previous estimates. Obviously, the records of past performances must be supplemented by their methods if any accurate forecasting is to be attempted. Past performances are useful to forecasting mainly in discovering indices that may be used and in checking the results obtained by combining and weighing indices.

24. *Adjusting for competition.* -The factor of competition is important to market forecasting but it presents very little opportunity for quantitative measurement. Except in a very few cases, the individual business enterprise cannot measure its several market units with accurate statistical percentages that will represent the sales of each competitor. To be sure, some companies by reason other than contracts and the activity of their branch sales managers are able to make reasonably close estimates of the volume of business done by their competitors in particular trading areas. If the statistics of the national volume of business done that is being done by their competitors are available, considerable use can be made of these territorial estimates.

Usually, however, adjustments for competition cannot be determined exactly, and although care should be exercised in making them they will be somewhat arbitrary in most cases. The severity of competition will vary from territory to territory. This fact constitutes a sound reason why two trading areas having the same sales potentialities in all respects other than with reference to competition, should not be expected to produce the same amount of sales. An allowance must be made for competition even if that allowance is partially arbitrary.

Any method must give weight to the length of time that the particular company has been distributing its products to a trading area, to the aggressiveness and efficiency of the company's own salesmen in the field, and to the degree of advertising support given to the salesmen. In addition, periodic surveys by means of personal interviews with representative distributors in a trading area will provide some basis for estimating the strength of competition.

25. *The market index.* -From the very beginning of experimentation with market forecasting there has been a widespread search for specific measuring sticks of market possibilities which correspond with variations in sales. If a direct relation can be found between a specific set of statistics and the company's market, the specific set of statistics is called a market index and may be used to indicate market potentialities. Even in cases where the exact nature of the casual relationship between the index statistics and the market potentialities is not known, any relationship that can be established and occasionally checked may be put to practical use in forecasting. A considerable amount of trail-and-error experimentation may be necessary, of course, before sound indices are discovered. The nature of the product line has a great deal to do with the relative difficulty in discovering market indices. The manufacturer of automobiles, for instance, meets almost immediately the suggestion of automobile registration as a possible index. The seller of electrical appliances has data available on the numbers of wired homes. However, the manufacturer of a kerosene-oil cooking stove may not be able to discover a suitable index with equal ease. In any circumstance, of course, apparent indices must be

considered merely tentative until some relationship between them and the product's market is discovered.

26. *No single and uniform index is useful.* -Many business enterprises adopt and use indiscriminately a single market index such as population, or magazine or daily newspaper circulation, or income tax returns. But no single measure will do for all commodities. As a rule, no single market index will be sufficient to measure accurately the potential market for any individual commodity. It is necessary usually to discover several factors that actually affect the sale of the individual commodity. How to discover these factors and how to use them in combination will be discussed in Chapter X. Finally, it should be stated that a proved market index or combination of indices can be used by themselves only to forecast the potential market of the industry in various territories. The method of using indices does not predict the market possibilities for the individual company. The percentage of these market possibilities for the industry which can be obtained by a given company must be determined by an arbitrary percentage adjustment for competition.

MARKET FORECAST METHODS

1. *Characteristics of a practical market index.* -The technique of market forecasting is concerned very largely with methods of singling out market indices, determining the effect each index really has, and combining the pertinent indices into a single measure, giving each component part its correct weight so that a reasonably accurate measure of sales possibilities may be obtained. The first of these problems should be handled on some basis other than mere seeming relationships between the apparent index and actual sales. A good market index should possess the following general characteristics:

(a) It should be based upon facts that are connected actually in some way with the given company's product line

(b) It should be sufficiently selective to eliminate the non-users of the company's products

(c) It should consist of a set of statistics that are accurate

(d) It should consist of up-to-date figures

(e) It should present the possibility of an economical compilation.

2. *Need of testing proposed indices.* -The process of finding actual relationships between tentative indices and the company's sales is, in most cases, a process of trial-and-error experimentation. Apparent connections between an individual set of statistics and sales must be tested and analyzed. In many cases coincidental market indices may seem to maintain a certain ratio to the company's sales, but these apparently connections may break down when they are examined carefully. In order to find factors which, correspond with variations in sales by

districts or trading areas it is desirable to us statistical methods of comparison. By such methods it can be discovered whether the suggested market index or factor actually moves along parallel with the variations of sales, or whether the two sets of data move in opposite directions.

3. *Methods of testing market forecast indices*. -Methods have been developed for testing forecasting indices. Some of these methods involve mathematical calculations. The most convenient as well as the most accurate statistical method of testing and expressing the connection between the two sets of data is by means of a coefficient of correlation. By working out the coefficient of correlation between a proposed index, such as number of income tax returns, for example, and the company's actual sales, trading area by trading area, the proposed index can be scientifically tested. If it shows high percentage of agreement with sales it can be adopted and used in combination with other indices which have been tested in the same way. If it does not show a close agreement with sales, it should be discarded as an indicating possibility. The various formulas for finding the coefficient of correlation between two set of measuring data are presented and discussed in practically all of the standard works on statistics. They are too specialized for presentation here. As a matter of fact, any business concern which wishes to set up a forecasting system should call upon an experienced market consultant to work out technique of the system.

4. *Important considerations in testing indices*. -In addition to this testing of suggested indices to establish their connection with the company's sales, these suggested indices should be examined to discover whether or not they meet the other requirements listed in an earlier chapter. The selectivity of the index may be evaluated qualitatively and may indicate that more than the particular index is necessary. Income tax statistics, for example, are probably of little selective value in excluding non-users in the case of a product line that sells over the retail counter at a price less than one dollar. Some attention, too, should be given to the probable accuracy of a set of figures which it is proposed to use as an index. If the source and method of collecting the statistics that make up a single possible index are at all open to question, it must be used with utmost caution. The question of frequent revisions and the current accuracy of the index factor must be taken into consideration. Many governmental compilations are almost out of date by the time they are issued. Finally, the cost of preparing and compiling periodically the several index factors must be estimated. If the process of forecasting becomes too complicated and costly, there may be a real question as to its value to the company.

5. *Commonly used market indices*. -Some of the most commonly used indices are:

(a) Population

(b) Income tax returns

(c) Value-of product indices

(d) Number of automobiles

(e) Number of telephones

(f) Trade indices such as bank deposits, building permits, etc.

(g) Magazines and newspaper circulation

(h) Number of retail outlets

This list is, of course, by no means exhaustive and represents only a few of the more commonly used indices. In every few cases, the individual seller will have to test these factors as suggestions and discover whether one or more can be used for his particular business. If these indices are of no value a search must be made for others that present an abundance of data and which are connected with sales. Each one of these indices listed will have quite definite limitations when used alone. A few words of comment are necessary with respect to each.

6. *Population*. -In the case of product lines that have a universal appeal, population is frequently considered to be an important market index. But unadjusted population figures used alone are misleading. Differences in wage rates and buying habits over the various trading areas make such an index an inaccurate guide.

For example, if the Pacific Coast areas are accustomed to buying the product line more freely than is the case in other areas, the proportion of sales on the Pacific Coast is definitely affected. Likewise, population statistics will give too high an estimate for areas where there are only a few people with high incomes and too low an estimate where there are many people with high incomes.

As a result of this inadequacy of unadjusted population figures for the native white population figures, negroes and foreigners are often excluded and the figures for the native white population are used. But even such an exclusion, while it will reduce the figures for New England, the Middle Atlantic, and Southern states it will increase slightly the other sections, will not make any material changes in the distribution figures. Certainly, the native white population index carries no guarantee of interpreting and measuring buying habits. Nor will the distribution of the literate population over 21 years of age prove to be a factor of any greater value as a general rule.

Illiteracy is unevenly distributed and there is a marked tendency of the larger cities to attract members of the age group above 21. It would be folly, for instance, for a manufacturer of linoleum to reply to any considerable extent upon literacy statistics as a market index.

7. *Income tax returns*. -The most obvious guide to purchasing power is that of income tax returns. But income tax returns are only a partial guide. Only about 6 per cent of the population have been paying an income tax. Large groups of the population do not earn incomes high enough to be required to make returns and other groups make their incomes from tax-exempt securities and other items of a similar nature. In fact, the market for most consumer's goods lies

to a great extent among people whose incomes are not represented in income tax returns. Moreover, an income totaling $3,500 in a city like New York is not the same as an income of $3,500 in Walhalla, North Dakota. The differences in the cost of living is all in favor of Walhalla. A comparison of income tax returns and population figures indicates that a much heavier percentage of income tax returns comes from the Pacific Coast than the population figures seem to warrant. The number of income tax returns alone, therefore, is hardly a selective or accurate market measure. If, on the other hand, some technique of adjustment can be worked out for average income, income range, and cost of living, area by area, the results should show the "length, width and depth per capita purchasing power."

8. *Value-of-price indices.* -Among the most important of the varied value-of-products indices are:

(a) The value of manufactured products

(b) The value of farm crops

(c) The value added by manufacture

(d) The value of mineral products

(e) The value of fishery products.

Most of these statistics are obtained from governmental departments such as the United States Census Bureau, in its Censes of Manufactures, the department of Commerce, the Geological Survey and Bureau of Fisheries. Like the income-tax statistics, those figures are often out of date before they are made available. Furthermore, the value indices are limited to various sections of the country and tend to overemphasize geographical centers of production.

In a given section, too, the value of manufactured products may be high because they are turned out by power-driven machinery under mass production methods, while the workers may be relatively few and earning only low wages. In another section where less of the work is done by machinery a larger number of workers may be employed and the total purchasing power of the area may be large, while the value of manufactured products may be low. Moreover, the value indices do not show necessarily that the value added has been accumulated in the particular area or how it has been added. Profits may go to few or to as many inside or outside of the particular area in which they are earned.

9. *Automobile registrations.* -Automobile registrations are also frequently used as a market index. It is possible to obtain statistics on the total number of each make sold in each county. But unless the product line has a very close relationship to the sale of automobiles, it is not apparent that automobile registrations constitute a good market index. When compared with income figures the automobile registrations for New England and the Middle Atlantic states are

low while through the east and west North-Central states the figures are astonishingly high. The Curtis Publishing Company in its "Sales Quotas" said:

Automobile registrations emphasize rural markets. In rural districts an automobile is generally recognized to be a necessity; in the city many who have the means to buy are deterred by lack of garage facilities and the congestion of city traffic.

It is difficult if not impossible to distinguish between automobiles that are purchased as necessities and those bought for pleasure. Nor do the statistics make any distinction between the new and used cars. Moreover, it is difficult to know which areas are thoroughly "worked" by the automobile manufacturer's and which are not. In general, it is perhaps safe to say that because pf installment buying, the ownership of automobiles is much less reliable as a market index to the manufacturer of a product line unrelated to automobiles than formerly was the case.

10. *Telephones*. -Statistics with respect to the number of telephones are frequently considered of value as market indicators. They can be obtained easily but they are confines to the basis of the state and the city of 50,000 population or over. Even if they were obtainable by counties, it is doubtful whether or not they would serve as accurate measures in many instances. Their ability to measure purchasing power is impaired by the effect of variations in rates, habits, sizes of cities, homogeneity of populations, and other factors. Telephone rates are relatively lower in small towns than in large cities because the limited number of subscribers cuts down the service demands. In small town, however, because of the homogeneity of the people, many families will not feel the need for telephones. In the large city, the lack of many personal acquaintanceships, the demand for rapid communication and the habit of ordering goods by telephone will promote telephone installations. The number of telephones may indicate families rather than individuals, but in the apartment-house cities such will not necessarily be the case. Cities will differ considerably one from the other in the number of telephones as compared with either the number of families or of individuals.

11. *Indices of trade activity*. -There are numerous groups of statistical indicators of trade activity that are sometimes used as market indices. Such figures as bank deposits, bank clearings, savings bank deposits, and building permits may be classed as trade indices. Total bank deposits present their particular weakness as market indicators. In the first place, the figures for bank deposits cannot be secured for all cities. In the second place, bank deposits include both checking accounts and savings accounts. Even the checking accounts are distorted by corporate and unit store deposits. Finally, banks receive deposits from wide surrounding areas particularly in rural and suburban sections. The received deposits cut across county lines- an individual county may show considerably more bank deposits than actually originate within its boundaries. Some of the same objections arise in the use of bank clearings as a market index. The corporate and unit store distortion is present as in the case of bank deposits. Moreover, duplication exists because the same check may be cleared at a number of different clearing points.

Savings bank deposits indicate something with respect to purchasing power. But they actually show the frugality of the depositors as well as their net purchasing power. Once a savings is made it is seldom withdrawn for the purchase of convenience or shopping goods. Thus, in a sense, savings bank deposits show where money is rather than where it is being or will be spent. So far as building permits are concerned it is evident that such figures may be important to manufacturers of product lines which are used in new building construction. But in the case a product line which is not directly related to the building trades it is hard to see any real service that this index may render of itself.

12. *Magazine circulation studies.* -The circulation statistics of various magazines are also used frequently as market indices. But circulation figures are hardly fundamental market factors. They are merely imperfect reflectors of market possibilities. When magazine circulation is used in combination with population figures, the influential population factor is duplicated in each index. When used alone, circulation figures present the question of what particular magazine circulation data should be used. In the various territories there is a marked variation in the circulation of different magazines. If circulation data really indicates buying power and buying tendency, there is always remaining the difficult question of selecting the magazine which best indicates these matters. The experiments in combining the circulation of several leading magazines have not resulted in the formulation of an accurate market index. One such index which combines the circulation of 30 national magazine shows only five per cent of circulation in New York State. Yet New York has at least ten per cent of the population and an even higher percentage of the purchasing power. The fact that illiterate or foreign born people do not subscribe to American national magazines does not bar them from the markets as purchasers of staple and fancy foods. In fact, in the case of butter, the very diet of groups of people like these may cause them to use more butter per capita than similar sized groups of literate and native-born consumers.

13. *Number of retail outlets.* -Occasionally, the number of retail outlets per capita basis is used as a market index on the theory that such statistics reflect the demand for goods. However, the figures for retail stores are far from accurate and they do not measure accurately the amount of business actually done at retail in particular territories. It is evident that one area may produce sales 100 per cent greater than another area and yet not support any more retail establishments. Nor do retail outlets indicate at all directly the net purchasing power of the ultimate consumers in those areas.

14. *Necessity for several indices.* -From this discussion of the limitations of some of the most commonly used market indices it should be clear that in almost every case accurate market forecasting will necessitate the use of more than one index. When several market indices are found which have a decided relation to the territorial variation in the sales of a particular commodity, the next task is to give each one of these market factors its proper weight and to combine them all into one single index. This task is by no means an easy one. In practice, the weighting of individual indices is accomplished mainly by estimating the relative weights.

15. *Suggested methods for weighing and combining indices.* -One interesting method of weighting indices arbitrarily was explained by Nelson Seubert, consulting statistician, in the

Editor and Publisher. Mr. Seubert discussed three market indices: The percentage distribution of population, the percentage distribution of the number of all income tax returns, and the percentage distribution of income tax returns on incomes of $10,000 and more. The first of these market indices he called the "quantity factor," the second, the "quality factor," and the third, the "luxury factor." To indicate the methods of weighting these indices, Mr. Seubert set up a six-fold classification of products having a universal appeal and suggested the proper weighting for each. They appear as follows:

Class 1. Cheap necessities and bulk staples. Weighting: Quantity factor 90 per cent. Quality factor 10 per cent. The great weight is logically given to population, but the amount of money available for purchases always affects the situation; hence the 10 per cent weighting given to income.

Class 2. Moderate-priced necessities and packaged staples. Weighting: Quantity factor 70 per cent. Quality factor 30 per cent.

Class 3. Quality-priced necessities and staples. Cheap luxuries and low-priced nonstaples. Weighting: Quantity factor 50 per cent. Quality factor 50 per cent.

Class 4. Fancy-priced necessities and staples. Moderate-priced luxuries and nonstaples. Weighting: Quantity factor 30 per cent. Quality factor 70 per cent.

Class 5. Quality-priced luxuries and nonstaples. Weighting: Quantity factor 10 per cent. Quality factor 90 per cent.

Class 6. Fancy-priced exclusive luxuries of high unit value. Weighting: Quantity factor 10 per cent. Exclusive luxury factor 90 per cent.

16. *Weighting and combining basic indices.* -Another equally interesting method of combining and weighting indices in the case of forecasting procedure used in estimating the wholesale and jobbing market for electrical supplies was reported by Edmund E. Lincoln, while economist for the International Telephone and Telegraph Company, in an article in the *Management Review*. In this instanced basic and variable indices were used. The basic market factors are those that have a steady growth in given territories, "so that within a reasonable period of time relationships between different territories, based on these factors, will probably not change appreciably." The particular basic indices which were selected were: Urban white population, population in territories served by central stations, value of production added by manufacture (all industries), central station capacity, residence meters, total horsepower of industrial plants, capitalization of industrial plants manufacturing electrical materials or products incorporating electrical materials, number of telephone stations not owned by Bell System, railroad mileage and passenger cars. These market factors were combined by arbitrary weightings into a composite basic factor index.

17. *Weighting and combining variable indices.* -The next step was the selection of "variable" market indices, those factors that are very sensitive sales indicators so far as the market for electrical goods in the various districts is concerned, "currently and from year to year." The particular "variable" factors chosen were: Building permits as compiled by Dun &

Bradstreet, production of electrical energy and bank debits outside of New York. The next bit of procedure was to weight and combine the two composite basic factor and one for the composite variable factor.

18. *Weighting often a matter of judgement.* -Throughout these procedures, the weighting of the various factors is a matter of judgement based on past experience and on sales possibilities relative to various classes of customers. In many cases such judgements are relatively sound. For instance, in the make-up of the composite variable factor a 50 per cent weighting is given to the index of building permits. Obviously, a very large per cent of the sales of electrical supplies are directly or indirectly influenced by new building activities.

19. *New experiments in weighting.* -Although in present practice indices are weighted and combined on the basis of empirical judgement alone, a considerable amount of experimentation is directed toward the use of mathematical and statistical methods to give each market factor its proper weight. The so-called statistical method of "multiple correlation" is growing in uses because it actually accomplishes an automatic and proper weighting in combination.

20. *Adjusting for competition.* -Finally, it should be said again that although the total sales of a given product line, territory by territory, can be determined by a reliable composite market index, the percentage of this market which can be obtained for a particular company depends upon the strength of the competition. Once the total potentialities are estimated, it is necessary to examine the particular competitive shares of the business which has been obtained by the company in the past and to rely upon such data in predicting the sales possibilities for the individual company. Of course, the percentage of share which has been secured in the past may be combined with a reasonable "percentage of encroachment" on competition. But this latter percentage, although arbitrarily set, must be determined with great caution. It must be determined in the light of the conservative opinion of the company's sales executives, the efficiency of present and proposed sales methods in the various territories, and the expected efficiency of the competitors' sales methods in the same territories. Obviously, the last factor is exceedingly hard to predict. Market forecasting is a particularly precarious undertaking when it comes to making adjustments for competition.

Lecture 4

PRODUCT POLICIES-FUNDAMENTALS

1. *Marketing policies*. -After market forecasting methods have been established the next step necessary is a consideration of the task formulating general marketing policies. A policy is a line or course of action predetermined for the purpose of insuring uniformity and consistency of procedure over a considerable period of time under recurrent and essentially similar circumstances. Generally, the attempt should be made to establish marketing policies for considerable periods of time. Changes should not be made without good reason. To be successful, policies must be followed definitely, and applied impartially. However, common sense must be used in their application.

A classification of general marketing policies, to be useful, must rest upon the basic factors with which particular policies are concerned. Marketing policies may be grouped as: Product policies, price policies, trade channel policies, and dealer and customer policies.

2. *Type of product to be manufactured*. -The first product policy of importance deals with the general type of product to be manufactured and marketed. While most medium-size or large manufacturing enterprises make and sell a line of products, it is entirely possible and often advisable to place the emphasis upon a particular type of product. The manufacturer who chooses to produce only convenience goods, or only shopping goods, or only specialty goods, definitely simplifies his problem of marketing. Nor does such a policy of limitation of product type preclude the possibility of building up a "line" of products which will include many different items of varying sizes, styles, and models. Some degree of emphasis on convenience goods, shopping goods, or specialty goods is highly profitable as a matter of product quality.

3. *Quality of the product line*. -Usually there is a demand for many different qualities of a particular product. The manufacturer should decide roughly on a high, medium, or low quality line. There is ample justification for a policy fixing on any one of these qualities. On the other

hand, it may be deemed advisable to make and sell several qualities of the same line. It is not unusual in manufacturing for two or more grades to result from the general process. In such cases, a policy of marking imperfect goods as "seconds" and of developing or reaching the markets for seconds may be adopted. Where several qualities of the same line are manufactured, the question of branding and of trade-channel policy are important. For instance, it may be desirable to use a brand name only in the first-quality products and to market other grades unbranded or in bulk. Or it may be wise to organize subsidiary companies or special departments to market the medium and low grades through trade channels other than those that are used for the high-grade products.

Definite policies with respect to quality are particularly desirable because of the difficulty of changing quality once a brand name has been identified with a particular product. After a quality reputation has been established for a particular product. After a quality reputation has been established for a particular product and its special brand name, it is always dangerous to lower the quality of the brand. Of a competitive necessity for a lower quality product appears, it is part of wisdom to issue a new and inferior product under a new brand name rather than to lower the quality of the old product under its old brand name.

4. *Style in relation to quality*. -The question of a product policy dealing with style is important. This question can hardly be considered apart from the question of quality. The important decision concerns the relation of style to quality and *vice versa*. In the case of most shopping goods, fashion or style is an important purchasing consideration. This type of merchandise appears to be especially subject to rapid shifts in the particular fashions or styles demanded by the ultimate consumer. The manufacturer must adopt some definite policy regarding the emphasis he will place upon style or fashion. If he makes shopping goods in the main, and decides that his emphasis is to be 30 per cent on quality and 70 per cent on style, he must be prepared to make sudden changes or adaptations in his product. If he manufactures convenience goods, he may perhaps, adopt a policy which is just the reverse of the above in emphasis. Good profit margins are essential. Whatever the natural inclination of the management must be made in a way to give the public what it wants.

5. *Competitive considerations*. – When decisions regarding type, quality, and style or fashion have been made, the product line should be analyzed from the point of view of competitive adaptation. Policies may be adopted that will set up exclusive competitive features. Emphasis may be placed on a special product element as the RCA Manufacturing Company has done with opera records. Additional and special features may be added to the product, such as the autographic device attached to the Eastman Kodak. The product may be simplified as in the case of the button less union suits and starch less collars.

6. *The number of articles to be manufactured*. -The manufacturer must also predetermine his general product policy regarding the number of articles to be produced. He must decide whether he will specialize in one article, whether he will attempt to make a full line, or family of products, or whether he will adopt a middle course. On this question no general rule can be laid down. Many successful business enterprises have been built upon the one-product policy. Others have been highly successful in marketing a family of products. Decisions must be made

only after a careful consideration of production costs and of the market. In many instances, a family of products of the same general type (convenience goods, or shopping goods, or specialty goods) can be marketed by the field sales force as easily as one item can be sold. If the products are naturally related, like "Heinz 57 Varieties" and the "National Biscuit" and "Sunshine" items ad if the retail outlets are all the same for all the individual members, the family policy may be quite profitable.

7. *Limitations on family-of-products lines.* -The family-of-products policy, however, can easily be carried too far. Natural relationships usually should not be overstepped, nor should an attempt be made to manufacture and sell a family of products if the markets for the suggested products are so widely different ass to necessitate separate sales forces for each market, unless this plan is necessary for other reasons that are particularly sound. Likewise, it should be remembered that if a family-of products policy loads down the manufacturer's salesmen with too many products he certainly cannot be a specialty salesman on each and every one. His task cannot be allowed to become the complicated task of the salesman for the general jobber.

8. *Diversification versus simplification.* -Closely connected with the preceding question of policy is the matter of sizes, models, and styles. It may be desirable to operate on a policy of simplification, or the limiting of the number of sizes, models and styles produced, and standardization. On this point there is likely to be considerable friction between the sales department and the manufacturing department. Salesmen like to work along the lines of least resistance. Consequently, they expect some pressure in the direction of a product line which offers many different sizes and styles.

The manufacturing executives, on the other hand, are almost certain to be committed to the theory that efficiency comes with a policy of standardized mass production. Hence they dislike to see much diversity in the product line. Generally speaking, the policy of simplification and standardization is profitable. Its general advantages include:

(a) Lower production costs

(b) Lower marketing costs

(c) Improved quality

(d) Improved service

(e) Reduced price

(f) Higher wages

Against these advantages must be measured the limitations of specialization. In the main, they are: Decreased sales, neglect of dealer's full needs, and sales monotony. Certainly, it is safe to say that in the case of product line, the purchase of which need not or perhaps should not involve the individuality and personal preference of the buyer, simplification and standardization may be extremely advisable. The manufacturer or producer of fabricating goods or accessory goods can very often make an effective use of this principle. However, in the case of consumer's goods, it should be remembered that the ultimate consumer is consciously extending taste and style as purchasing factors. Consumer demand is the governing influence and if that demand involves the possibility of choosing from a varied assortment of styles and sizes, the policy of simplification should not be carried too far.

9. *The guarantee.* -Another matter that has a direct reference to the product line and that should be expressed in a predetermined policy is the matter of guarantee. In the earlier days of marketing history, the guarantee was little known and used. The common law developed the business maxim of *caveat emptor*, let the buyer beware. To-day, however, very few reputable manufacturers are willing to hide behind this seeming legal justification of unsound practices. The manufacturer or distributor who does not in some degree guarantee the things he sells is decidedly the exception.

10. *Implied or expressed guarantees.* -In most cases, the modern purchaser assumes an implied guarantee that he will be able to secure services from the manufacturer of a particular product line such as he can expect reasonably when price is taken into account. Naturally, the implied guarantee has distinct limitations. It does not bind the house.

Nevertheless, the ultimate consumer usually will expect a reputable concern to deliver goods as represented, and to make adjustments if the goods do not prove to be as represented. This situation will exist unless there is an expressed statement to the contrary or unless no representations are made and the goods are marked "seconds" or manufacturer's rejects." Generally speaking, the expressed guarantee is desirable because it adds slightly more definiteness to an inevitable implication which may be stretched very far by the unscrupulous purchaser. As a business builder, no other policy is more effective than an expressed guarantee which binds the seller to stand behind his goods.

11. *Limited performance guarantees.* -It is advisable to determine whether or not the expressed guarantee should be limited or unlimited. It may be desirable, for example, to limit the expressed guarantee to particular features of performance. When a manufacturer if automobile tires agrees to replace a tire which fails, at a cost of one-twelfth of its original price, for every month it has been used, up to 12 months, he is offering a guarantee of performance.

The same would be true of a manufacturer of electric washing machines who guarantees for certain districts that, barring an increase in rates, the cost of electricity for operating the machines will not exceed two cents per hour. Obviously, performance may be measured in terms of time as well as wear or costs. An automobile manufacturer who guarantees his crankshaft against breakage for two years is also issuing a performance guarantee. This type of guarantee is usually highly explicit and specific in statement. It has the advantage of limiting adjustment if the product is absolutely right with respect to the detailed performance guaranteed.

12. *The limited guarantee of quality.* -The limited guarantee of quality is generally less specific and definite than the limited guarantee of performance. It is naturally more general because it attempts to make a broad statement that will develop confidence in the quality of an article as a whole. When the automobile tire manufacturers began to use guarantee against

imperfections in their goods rather than a mileage guarantee, they substituted a quality guarantee for a performance guarantee. When the washing machine manufacturer offers a bond that guarantees his product against all imperfections in workmanship and material for a period of one year, a time limitation appears. The guarantee is similar to that of the automobile manufacturer who guarantees his car against mechanical defects for 90 days. Because of the general character of the quality guarantee, a fool-proof product line is necessary, and usually it is the part of wisdom to set up some specific time limitation.

13. *Unlimited guarantees.* -An unlimited guarantee policy may also be used although in most cases it is open to considerable abuse by the ultimate consumer. "The customer is always right" has been applied as a slogan by many retail establishments, and some, at least, have lived up to the letter of the slogan with apparent profit. Generally speaking, an unlimited guarantee is somewhat dangerous when the product is complex and demands a considerable degree of skill in its operation. When an unlimited guarantee has been expressly indicated, it is exceedingly difficult to do anything else but make complete restitution, even when breakdown is due to conscious or unconscious carelessness in operation.

14. *The mail-order guarantee.* -The mail-order house is perhaps the chief user of the unlimited guarantee. One well-known Chicago concern uses the following statement:

We guarantee that every article in this catalog is honestly described and illustrated. We guarantee that any article purchased from us will give full and complete service. If for any reason whatever you are not satisfied with any article purchased from us, we want you to return it to us at our expense. We will then exchange it for exactly what you want or will return your money, including any transportation charges you have paid.

This type of retail institution needs a strong and all-inclusive guarantee to develop complete confidence on the part of the ultimate consumer and to influence him to buy or mail. On the average, the mail-order customer will not abuse the privilege of adjustment to the same extent as will the customer of a retail store located in his own trading area. It is a good deal of trouble to return articles in the first case, and extremely easy in the second.

15. *The guarantee of the distributor.* -Whatever the type of guarantee that may be decided upon, the manufacturer must outline his policy of standing behind his distributors in cases of complaints or of request for adjustment under the guarantee. For example, if the guarantee contains a money-back provision, in most cases some arrangement should be made with the distributor so that an ultimate consumer can receive his money back from the distributor from whom he purchased the goods without waiting for the article to be sent to the factory.

In cases where the product line is subject to deterioration or perishability, the matter of standing behind the dealer may be of special importance. In the sale of candy, prepared foods, yeast, and the like, it will be almost necessary to provide a liberal replacement policy to distributors in case of deterioration through the delay in delivery, or even in the case of delay in sale by the wholesaler or retailer. Of course, any policy of standing behind the dealer must be administered with exceeding care. If the manufacturer is excessively liberal in making adjustments to the distributors, they, in turn, may grow careless in checking up the statements made by their customers who complain.

16. *Service policies*. -Finally, the manufacturer must predetermine his product policy from the standpoint of service. Service may mean a continuing interest in the customer after he has purchased the goods. It may mean real helpfulness preceding the sale, with the purpose of fitting the product to the customer's particular needs. In some cases, it implies offering assistance and information in matters only indirectly connected with the seller's goods. Occasionally it may mean nothing at all. There is considerable talk about service which begins and ends in conversation alone. It is easy to over-sell service. It is probably never possible to over-serve.

In general, service, as the word is properly applied in modern business, means giving the buyer something more than so many yards, or so many pounds, or so many units in exchange for the market price. It means the doing of things that increase the comfort, convenience, and happiness of the buyer, and increase his goodwill towards the seller. A policy of real service, is a policy of enlightened selfishness. The buyer pays, of course, for all that he gets, whether there is placed at his disposal a service station, a rest room, a repair part service, or the skill of the manufacturer's engineers. But he is often better pleased to pay for a product with service than he would be to buy the bare product at a lower price. The right kind of service is not expensive but it makes sales. No manufacturer or seller can well afford to omit service of some kind from his product policy.

PRODUCT POLICIES-IDENTIFICATION

1. *The value of a good name*. -In business, what is the value of a good name? Manufacturers of certain products known the world over value the identification marks, such as brand names, on their goods at a million dollars a letter. But is it worthwhile for most manufacturers to adopt an identification policy? Is it profitable to adopt a name, sigh, or symbol by means of which consumers will know that a particular commodity is the product of a certain maker? The magnitude and the complexity of modern business seem to make necessary the adoption of some identification policy, the use of brand to connect in the consumer's mind the product with its maker. What are some of the factors which dictate the adoption of such a policy? The success of certain well-known commodities is only one factor. There are others which seem to dictate that the great majority of products should be in some matter identified.

2. *Competition and advertising demand branded goods*. -Two of these factors are evident to the most casual observer: The increase in competition, and the growth of advertising. Competition has brought forth a myriad of products in many different lines. Some method of identification is required to distinguish one from the other. As soon as a single manufacturer brands his product, others making the same type of commodity must do likewise. Competition is

further increased by the struggle to maintain brand leadership. A further stimulus to this competition and a factor in itself in making some sort of product-identification necessary, it is the tremendous growth I advertising of all kinds. The maker of a commodity who advertises to the consumer is forced to adopt and exploit a brand to identify his product.

3. *Consumers have become brand-conscious.* -The working of these forces has made the consumer brand-conscious to the point where many purchasers buy, not products, but brands. This consciousness has been accentuated by the appearance of many commodities for widespread and everyday use which are highly technical in construction: The automobile, radio, electric refrigerator and scores of appliances that most of us use and know little about in detail. The consumer, because of his lack of special knowledge, can form no prepurchase judgment as to the quality of the product or its fitness for his needs. Hence, he buys either on the basis of good will toward the individual dealer or confidence in the maker of the product. *If the product is unbranded, the consumer cannot identify it with its maker.* To meet growing competition, to make the most of advertising, the up-to-date manufacturer who is at all directly dependent on consumer buying must adopt an identification policy, must brand his product.

4. *Results identification may accomplish.* -Before deciding what form or combination of forms of identification he will use, the maker of the product should clearly recognize what results he may hope to realize from such a policy. An identification mark may call from the consumer three distinct responses: Consumer recognition, consumer preference, and consumer insistence. A consumer will normally select from a shelf some article whose identification mark he has somewhere previously noted, on a package or in an advertisement. The number of products bought on the basis of price or style rather than by brand is constantly decreasing. Preference is stronger than recognition. A consumer who prefers a product sufficiently to ask for it by its brand name or other identification mark, will not accept a substitute product without objection. The third effect, insistence, is achieved if the purchaser will accept no substitute. Tests have proved that brand consciousness of widely advertised commodities has been highly developed. Arrow collars, Eastman Kodaks, and O'Sullivan rubber heels are cases in point.

5. *The four identification forms.* -If the manufacturer decides that the achieving of these responses or effects is worthwhile in the case of his product, he must then choose the form or forms of identification he will use. There are four common forms of identification: The brand name, the trademark, the slogan, and the trade character. A product may be identified by one or more of these forms.

6. *The types of brand names.* -The brand name is merely a name which serves to identify, favorably if possible, the product. There are at least four well defined types of brands or trade names. As an identification mark, a brand name may be merely the name of the concern making the product, for example, "Goodyear" tires, "Buick" automobiles, or "Packer's" tar soap. The names may be taken form a geographical locality; "Canada Dry" ginger ale, "Cape Cod" cranberries, "Boston" garters are examples. In the third case, the name may supposedly reflect the quality of the product, as "Holeproof" hosiery, swift's "Premium" ham, or "Royal baking powder. Finally, the brand name may be catchy, artificially-created compound, as "Walk-Over," "Sunkist," or "Keen Kutter," or "7-Up."

7. *The characteristics of an effective brand name.* -An effective brand name must measure up to certain qualifications, the most important of which are:

(a) It should be easy to pronounce, spell, and remember. (Holeproof.)

(b) It should be distinctive, not easily confused with any other name. (Kodak.)

(c) It should be appealingly suggestive of the product and, if possible, of its use. (Keen Kutter, Adjusto-Lite.)

(d) It should comply with legal requirements. (Personal, geographical, or descriptive names cannot be registered.)

How highly an effective brand name is valued is evidenced by the elaborate efforts, often including prize contests, that are made to secure one.

8. *The marketing of more than one brand.* -A single brand is undoubtedly preferable for an entire line of products if all the products are similar and of equal quality. It is on this principle that food manufacturers often use a single brand name or family name for the whole line. "Heinz's 57" is a good example of a family of products. One brand name is also sufficient for the entire line if only one quality is manufactured, irrespective of the type of product. Certain circumstances, however, justify the use, by a manufacturer, of more than one brand name or trademark. Different brand names are used where different grades or qualities are made by the same producer; the products may even be competitive. A second brand is often used to meet price competition. The product sold under the regular brand name may not reach a sufficiently wide market. Competitors enter the field to take this market, often with goods of cheaper quality and hence of lower price. The manufacturer does not wish to cut the price on his first-quality brand; nor does he wish to fight the competition with a cheaper product under the same brand name. Hence, he makes a second brand, lower in price-sometimes not in quality-to meet the competition. This is often called a fighting brand. Again, an additional brand may be justified for marketing through outlets other than those regularly employed, that is, jobbers, chain stores and mail-order houses.

Can a single sales organization successfully handle two or more competing brands? Experience seems to have demonstrated that unless the organization is almost perfectly set up and manned, the practice is unsuccessful. However, the question is debatable; particular circumstances constitute an important factor. The General Motors Corporation maintains separate sales organizations for its different makes of automobiles. Remington Rand, Inc., on the other hand, has merged the selling forces of competing brands of its products.

9. *The trademark.* -Not infrequently the brand name is also used as the trademark. The trademark, however, may be something quite different: A design, a signature, the combination of a design and the brand name. a trademark made up wholly or in part of the design that gives a picture effect may be more valuable than just a brand name. There are innumerable illustrations

of the fine quality if trademarks: The "Dutch Boy" white lead, for paints; the "Dutch Girl" eternally chasing dirt, for a cleaner; the "Cream of Wheat Chef," for a breakfast food; the Dromedary Camel," for sweetmeats.

A number of tests have been made to determine the effectiveness of trademarks and their design. Psychologists have found, for example, that persons and faces are more easily remembered than objects, and that objects are less easily forgotten than actions; that form is more easily remembered and recognized than color, although colors are more accurately remembered than numbers. Recent tests show that the order of recognition and recall is: Pictures, forms, words, syllables.

10. *Qualifications of a trademark*. -The qualification of the trademark are much the same as those for the brand name, plus the additional quality of describability. The growth of packaging has made it especially essential that a trademark be of a design which one person can easily describe to another when recommending the purchase of the particular brand. This factor definitely increases stability; not infrequently, for example, a customer desiring "Dromedary" dates will ask for a package "with the picture of the camel on it." The use of trademarks on packages has made necessary designs that are simple, easily reproduced, easily recognized, easily explained, and that are at the same time colorful and attractive. To capitalize fully a trademark, wide advertising is, of course, required. Any reputable advertising agency can give suggestions as to the procedure. The registering of brand names and trademarks is a legal matter, and a competent attorney specializing in trademark and patent work should be consulted about the steps to be taken.

11. *Static versus flexible identification forms*. -The brand name and the trademark are virtually static forms of identification. Any changes in their use is difficult to make and runs the risk of general loss of value and of the forfeiture of legal protection of the mark.

Sometimes, however, changes are necessary; the design on the trademark of a soldier in the uniform of 1898 is now obsolete because a soldier is at present associated with the uniform of to-day. Civilian clothes, particularly feminine apparel, have changed almost as radically in the same period.

12. *The slogan*. -The slogan is a catch phrase, which by constant repetition stimulated by advertising, becomes associated with a certain product or its maker. "They Satisfy," "Have You a Little Fairy in Your Home?" "Ask the Man Who Owns One," "More miles per Gallon," are examples that have become famous. The good slogan should be more than a catch phrase; wherever possible it should give certain information about the product to intensify the desire for the product's use.

A slogan is often an expensive investment. Considerable advertising of a varied character is usually required to make people familiar with it so that they will connect it immediately with the product. If the slogan is changed-and its flexibility is supposedly one of its assets-a new advertising campaign is required. A slogan, furthermore, is difficult to register in the patent office due to its tendency to be less individual than a trademark and therefore not so much an item of private right. Faced with all these considerations, the manufacturer should use particular care in the choice of a slogan.

13. *Slogan polices.* -If a slogan is expected to last over a long period, it should be remembered that products contain and conditions change. A specific slogan may have to be changed accordingly. The slogan must also be rational. A discriminating public is becoming perhaps increasing critical. If so, it may ask whether virgin or reworked wool went into "The Cloth That Is 100% Wool," or demand to see the formula for soap that is 99.44/100% Pure." If a slogan cannot be made irrefutably rational, the emotional type may be more effective. The ideal emotional type may be more effective. The ideal emotional slogan appeals more to the pleasure which the consumer will enjoy while or after using the product. This type of slogan is exemplified by "They Satisfy," "The Flavor Lasts," and a host of phrases displayed by billboards, car cards, magazines and newspaper advertisements, or packages.

14. *The use of the trade character.* -A trade character is a humanized figure, tending sometimes towards the caricature, which symbolizes the product or its uses, or both. It is ordinarily employed in the place of, or as a supplement to a plain, fixed symbol. The fixed symbol is frequently used in connection with the brand name to make up the trademark. A trade character with an effective slogan may also be used as the trademark. "It Chases Dirt" is the phrase used, in connection with the Dutch Girl in the blue dress and carrying a stick, symbolizing one of the cleaning compounds. The combination is as well-known as any other trademark.

Trade characters can, of course, be highly animated and used in changed positions, like the Wrigley sprites. These features may take the trade character and identification form peculiarly suitable for certain products, even if used only as supplement to the regular trademark.

15. *Some disadvantages of flexible identification forms.* -The use of the trade character is often an effort to capitalize on people's desires for entertainment. They do watch good trade characters perform their antics. But does the entertainment thus furnished make purchasers of the spectators? If the trade character and the slogan are to be used flexibly-changed often-in advertising, they are likely to become costly forms of identification. Caution should be exercised in employing them. A particular word of warning must be given about the use of the trade character. An over-imaginative artist in creating and modifying the trade character may lean a bit too strongly towards caricature. People like humor-but humor tempered with a little dignity.